THE ROAD TO SELF-EMPLOYMENT

A Practical Guide to Microbusiness Development

By
GERRI P. NORINGTON

WOMEN'S BUSINESS
TRAINING CENTER &
KMN Growth Consultants

San Diego, California

THE ROAD TO SELF-EMPLOYMENT
A Practical Guide to Microbusiness Development

By
GERRI P. NORINGTON

Copublished by
Women's Business Training Center &
KMN Growth Consultants
P.O. 126305
San Diego, CA 92112-6305
(619) 239-9282 voice
(619) 238-5205 fax

© Copyright 1997 by Gerri P. Norington

ALL RIGHTS RESERVED. No part of this publication may be
reproduced, stored in a retrieval system or transmitted in any form
or by any means electronic, mechanical, photocopying, recording or
otherwise, without the prior written permission of the publisher.

Cover Design: J. Bird Design
Publication Layout & Design: J. Bird Design

Library of Congress Catalog Card Number: 97-60414
ISBN: 1-890499-00-5

1st Printing
March 1997

Printing:
Bayport Press, Chula Vista, California

DEDICATION

This work is dedicated
to all of my clients
—past, present and future.

A special dedication goes to
the women who have fought
the battles and paved the
way for those coming
behind them. May you
always be remembered for
the injustices you have
endured to level the playing
field, to the extent that it
has been leveled. May
women continue to strive for
economic independence.

Best Wishes
Gerri Norington

ACKNOWLEDGMENTS

My sincere thanks to Sue Lord for transcribing the sometimes jumbled tapes that led to this piece of work. She is masterful to have made sense of it. A special thanks to Linda Puig for her editorial expertise; she sometimes suffered indignities to work with me, in spite of which she did a great job. Jane Onstott also provided superb editorial assistance.

A huge debt of gratitude is owed Joyce Black of J. Bird Design. Her creative cover graphics and page layout have made this book a visual success before any were sold.

Thanks to Lee Fenn for his input on the financials and for his general support of the Women's Business Training Center. Thanks also to Sherry Martin, DeBorah Roy, Jon Bodnar, Karen Hurst-Warren and Meredith Nole for their eagle eyes in proofing, and to all the clients who have taught me so much about life and business development over the years.

An extra special thanks goes to Joni Halpern, attorney, friend and supporter. Finally, I thank Dennis Rohrig and Kevin Kelly, who, along with others, have provided the enduring support to get me through the sacrifices necessary to complete this book.

TABLE OF CONTENTS

THE ROAD TO SELF-EMPLOYMENT
A Practical Guide to Microbusiness Development

Introduction

As a business consultant, trainer and business coach since 1968, I have owned and operated five different businesses. In the course of those years, I have coached thousands of small business owners working hard to make their businesses successful. The one inevitable trait I encounter among many of them is the failure to understand or to accept the need to plan—to look ahead and map a course for where they want to go and for how to deal with the roadblocks and challenges that are bound to pop up.

I also came to realize that it takes a person to operate a business. I couldn't just provide technical business information without dealing with the aspects of a person's character that either hinder or enhance success. I developed a technique over the years that allows me to help people start to get in touch with themselves: their attitudes, fears, insecurities—all the things that affect how they operate as business people. I help them combine increased personal awareness with solid business development information to create a successful business operation.

This kind of assistance is more critical today than ever before. Huge numbers of people are going into business today. The economy is such that large companies are downsizing to compete with smaller, leaner companies, leaving many workers to their own devices. These smaller companies are able to earn a tremendous income without the heavy overhead larger corporations bear. By the year 2000, it is estimated that 80 percent of all workers in this country will work for small businesses with fewer than 50 employees. Small business owners will be responsible for nearly the entire economy.

Yet the federal Small Business Administration calculates that 90 percent of all small businesses fail within the first five years of operation. Those numbers are staggering and have not come down over the past 20 years. It's time that small and microbusiness owners stop, learn and understand what they need to do for a greater chance at business success—not just for themselves, either; the country is depending on it.

That's why I wrote this book: to help stem the high failure rate of small business owners across the country. The book is long overdue; I have planned to write it since 1982. It is my pleasure to bring you *The Road To Self-Employment: A Practical Guide to Microbusiness Development*. This step-by-step guide will help microbusiness owners understand how to achieve lasting success.

The book is divided into three sections. Section I is Preparing Yourself For The Trip. In this section, I talk about you as a prospective or current microbusiness owner. I teach you how to get in touch with what's going on inside. What is your attitude about life, about business? How do these attitudes affect how you do business? How can adjusting these attitudes help you run your business more effectively? With what kind of fears do you struggle? Awareness is the first critical step—and a huge one—that you need to take to be successful.

Section II is Preparing The Vehicle For The Trip. Here, we look at ways to make sure that your business is planned effectively, to give you a strong possibility of success in business.

Section III is Mapping Your Journey. In it, I help you to implement systems that will lead to your business success.

Throughout the book are exercises that I hope you will take the time to complete. These exercises help you think through the process of business development. Completing the exercises will heighten your level of comprehension. You spend too much time, money and energy on your business not to give it every chance of success.

This book is about empowerment. I want to empower you with the knowledge, ability and desire to be effective in operating your business. I hope that you will use the information in this book to break the barrier, becoming one of the 10 percent that succeed. Perhaps together we can raise that national success rate to at least 60 percent. **Here's to your success!**

SECTION I

- **PREPARING YOURSELF FOR THE TRIP**

CHAPTER ONE

Getting to Know Yourself

Looking Inside

Even with all the technology around us today, it still takes a person to run a business. A person with hopes, fears, dreams, insecurities, abilities, emotions. A person with an individual set of values and attitudes.

Trying to operate a business without taking into consideration your whole self is like baking a chocolate cake without chocolate. You've missed the defining trait, what makes the chocolate cake what it is. Who you are and how you operate matters. It matters to the success of the business and it matters to your enjoyment as an entrepreneur. Personal growth and development combined with nuts-and-bolts business information start you off on the right road to building a successful business operation.

I advocate and teach a holistic approach to developing a microbusiness that takes into consideration your whole self. It develops you as a person so that you can develop your business. When you get in touch with yourself, you discover that you can give your all to running a business and still maintain a healthy balance in your life. Your interactions will be more fruitful, your decisions more grounded, your dreams more tangible.

But first, what is a microbusiness? Microbusinesses have 10 or fewer employees, including the owner. Though some microbusinesses require larger amounts of start-up capital (up to several hundred thousand dollars), they generally require less than small businesses. We're talking as little as a few hundred dollars and, on average, several thousand dollars. While the information in this guidebook will help any business owner navigate the road of self-employment, the focus is on the microbusiness owner operating with less than $100,000.

YIELD

[handwritten margin note:] not sure from people + people not have to work for someone

Questions for Getting Started

As with any trip, the journey to self-employment begins with a question: "Where do you want to go?" And even more importantly: "Do you really want to take this trip? Is business development really for you?" Look around you. Understand what you're getting into before you take that first step of starting a business. Look inside yourself. Business ownership is not for everyone. I believe that an entrepreneur is born with a special spirit. Certainly there are people lacking that entrepreneurial spirit who can succeed, but without the right training, they generally don't stay in business as long. Without a realistic understanding of themselves, they're not likely to get back up after failing, dust themselves off and start another business. Are you an entrepreneur?

You need to answer these questions before you develop a business. Doing so helps you to understand what you bring to the business and what you want the business to bring to you. It helps instill a sense of direction and purpose. It shows you the areas on which you will need to work.

Today, with so many people being edged out of jobs, entrepreneurs are not the only ones thinking about business development. As director of the Women's Business Training Center, I regularly see clients—prospective business owners who have advanced degrees and have worked as employees for many years—now forced to start a business just to be employed. To have a job, they must create it. This situation, though unfortunate, is commonplace in today's economy and probably will be for years to come. That's the trend: self-employment. So if you're not an entrepreneur at heart, training and guidance are necessary to give you a better chance to succeed. You're going to need every skill, every advantage, every leg up on the competition.

Is business development really for you?

As you begin to ask yourself these critical questions, keep this in mind: You don't have to do it alone. In fact, it's best to work with an experienced coach, consultant or mentor who can offer suggestions, advice and guidance. It's not enough to attend a weekend workshop or a 10-day conference, or to sit down with a consultant once or twice. Regular contact regarding the day-to-day decisions and difficulties of running a business may make the difference between success and failure.

Self-Discovery Exercise

It is rare for people to be in touch with who they are, how they think and how they feel. Here is an exercise to help you get in touch with what's going on inside. Ponder your responses, as they'll help you understand how you really feel about yourself. Your honesty is critical. Be spontaneous—don't spend more than 30 seconds on each response. Don't use information about yourself, such as height, age, weight or occupation. Think more about qualities or personality characteristics. Complete the following sentences:

1. **I am...(Write five of these sentences.)**

2. **What I like most about myself is...**

3. **I wish I could...**

4. **I hate it that I...**

5. **I would like to change...**

6. **I do (don't) consider myself caring because...**

7. **Five adjectives that best describe me are:**

8. **Five things I really like about myself are:**

Now you can become more aware of how you think, how you feel, how you deal with people, and what you like and dislike about yourself. What are your "hot buttons? " What turns you on? What makes you angry? What do you do well?

First, focus on the things you dislike about yourself. Step outside yourself for a moment, as though you were another person, and use your creativity to design a better approach to dealing with situations. How can you evolve and begin to be more pro-active rather than reactive to situations and certain individuals?

Now, figure out how to enhance the things you like about yourself. They'll help you move forward in your business. What else empowers you to move forward? This book is an experiment in empowerment. I want to empower you with the knowledge, the ability and the desire to be successful in running your business.

Confronting Fears

Remember being afraid of monsters and bogeymen as a child? We adults have our own monsters and bogeymen associated with going into business and with life in general. To succeed in business, you'll have to confront these fears. That means first knowing what they are, bringing them out of that dark closet into the light of day.

Here's an exercise to help you identify your fears and understand how best to deal with them:

List and number all of your fears, especially those related to running a business. Complete the list over a period of several days; don't try to think of all of your fears in one sitting. Once you feel your list of fears is complete, review them. Ask yourself, for each fear, whether you can actually do anything about it. If the answer is yes, write that fear on another piece of paper. Create on that paper an action plan to help you get past the fear. It's not uncommon to have as many as 10 or 20 fears with which to reckon. Just remember: Fear is normal.

EXAMPLE: *Your fear is that you'll not make money in business. Examining this fear, you realize that it's unfounded and not terribly realistic. It has no basis other than fear itself. Your action plan to confront the fear might include learning as much as possible about the business you have in mind, completing financial projections that will tell you how much money you need to stay in business and developing marketing strategies that will allow you to generate the revenue necessary to keep the business going.*

Realize that you have the control and power to change how you think and how you feel.

Preparing financial projections and developing marketing strategies can reduce your fear of not making enough money. That's how it works. Examining your fear—and dealing with it constructively—helps you put it behind you. You come to realize that you have control over the situation. You must then be able to take control. Learn what you need to know to overcome the fear. Fear, then, can actually be positive in that it can motivate you to take action and move forward. Fear can also keep you from becoming overconfident, helping you to stay on track and prepare for what is to come. As long as fear is not debilitating, it's healthy.

Take charge! Realize that you have the control and power to change how you think and how you feel. Look at the fears you have listed and decide what actions you might take to overcome each.

Be aware that some fears, such as the fear of dying, are irrational; you can't do a whole lot about these fears. We're all going to die, but we don't know when it will happen. It's not something you have control over so don't dwell on it. Simply make the best use of your time while you are here. Change your way of thinking: rather than thinking about dying, focus on living. The present is all you can control, not the past or the future.

Values

What are values? They are internal conceptions—internal standards or qualities—of what is desirable and of what determines right from wrong. Families, organizations, companies, governments, and the individuals who comprise them all have values.

Understanding what your values are will better prepare you to deal objectively with your life and business. Knowing your values helps you be in touch with yourself. This awareness allows you to consciously determine the guiding principles by which you will run your life and your business. Awareness of your guiding principles facilitates decision making and consequently helps you to build a strong business and stay focused on your objectives. Self-awareness prepares you to function in the present, prepare for the future and not relive the past.

> **Values are one of the most important elements of life. They affect everything you do. The more you understand about your values, the clearer you can be in your ideas about life and the more confident you can be in your actions.**
>
> **Values are the silent power in personal and organizational life. Values are at the core of your personality, influencing the choices you make, the people you trust, the appeals to which you respond, the way you invest your time and energy. In turbulent times, values can give us a sense of direction amid conflicting views and demands.**
>
> **Values are the foundation of our character and of our confidence. There can be little happiness if the things you believe in are different from the things you do. They define you whether or not you are conscious of them. Having a clear understanding of your values and acting on them can lead to a clear life, relatively free from complications. When you are able to live according to your values, you receive the respect of others and of yourself.**

Printed with permission from Life Values, *by Karen A. Dietz, Ph.D.*[1]

[1] For additional information on values contact Karen A. Dietz, Ph.D, Polaris Associates, 12804 Amaranth St. San Diego, CA 92129, Phone: (619) 538-5254, Fax: (619) 538-5253 Email: tkd@cts.com

To help you better understand your values, complete the following exercise. For each of the four groups, divide the 21 values into three groups of seven, according to whether they are: A) most important, B) somewhat important or C) least important. Next, rank each group of seven in order of importance, with the first being the most important. For the moment, pay no attention to the codes beside each word.

Life Values—Global

Community (S) l
Freedom (P/S) l
Wisdom (P) sd
Health (P) l
Spirituality (P) sd
Nature (P/S) sr
Aesthetics (P) l
Pleasure (P) l
Love (S) r
Social Service (S) sr
Adventure (P) l
Family (S) r
Fellowship (S) r
Equality (S) r
Wealth (P) l
Fame (P) l
Power (P/S) l
Self-Worth (P/S) sd
Achievement (P) l
Peace (S) sr
Happiness (P) sd

Life Values—Operational

Fairness (M) sd
Order (C/M) c
Discipline (C/M) c
Courtesy (M) r
Flexibility (C) l
Courage (M) sd
Creativity (M) sd
Affection (M) r
Service (M) r
Humor (C/M) sd
Forgiveness (M) sr
Loyalty (M) c
Tolerance (M) sr
Obedience (M) l
Autonomy (C) i
Honesty (M) sr
Accountability (C) c
Competency (C) i
Drive (C) c
Reason (C) c
Knowledge (C) i

Legend to Values Exercise

LIFE VALUES

P = Personal. Focus on self and relate to individual alone.

S = Social. Focus on society and suggest involvement and importance of others.

C = Competence. Refers mainly to those values which, when compromised, produce feelings of personal inadequacy.

M = Moral. Refers to those values which produce pangs of conscience or a feeling of wrong-doing.

sr = social responsibility

i = influence

sd = self-development

r = relationships

c = continuity

l = lifestyle

Organizational Values— Cultural

Equality (R)

Integrity (T/R)

Leadership (R)

Harmony (R)

Achievement (T)

Innovation (T)

Customer (T/R)

Fun (R)

Efficiency (T)

Excellence (T)

Family (R)

Control (T)

Community (R)

Learning (R)

Growth (T)

Teamwork (R)

Safety (T/R)

Tradition (T/R)

Quality (T)

Profitability (T/R)

Empowerment (R)

Organizational Values— Operational

Independence (P)

Knowledgeable (P)

Loyalty (E)

Obedience (E)

Power (P)

Recognition (P/E)

Risk Taking (P)

Structure (P)

Versatility (P)

Compassion (E)

Diversity (E)

Cooperation (P)

Competition (P/E)

Communication (P)

Creativity (P)

Accountability (E)

Credibility (E)

Dependability (P/E)

Discipline (P)

Drive (P)

Fairness (E)

Legend to Values Exercise

ORGANIZATIONAL VALUES

T = Task. Enhance or empower the individual.

R = Relationship. Focus on relating to others, fostering involvement with the community.

P = Process. Refers to the "rightness" of an action with regards to effectiveness.

E = Ethical. Refers to "rightness" of an action with regards to standards of morality or propriety.

After ranking all the groupings, use the legends to examine each group, paying special attention to its classification. Notice any trends? Is there a pattern as to which values you hold most important, which principals and standards you will live by?

Think about how you manifest these values in your life—how you operate and how you deal with others. Being in touch with your values can guide you in organizing and running your business.

Attitudes

Carl Meninger once said, "Attitudes are more important than facts." Attitudes shape our lives and our values. They shape our effectiveness in interacting with people. They affect our health and every aspect of our being. Adjusting your attitude can change your health, the way in which people respond to you and how often you will succeed at a task.

Attitude is often a result of how you feel about yourself. Confidence normally breeds a positive attitude. Insecurity, fear, self-hatred, lack of confidence—these underlie a negative attitude and often make you afraid to assert yourself or cause others to respond negatively to you.

Attitude is often a result of how you feel about yourself.

Changing your attitude is not always easy. We are, after all, creatures of habit. It has taken a long time to cultivate the attitudes you have and it will take a conscious effort to change them. The first step is the desire to change, realizing that current attitudes are not moving you in the direction of choice. The key here is to function in the present, aware of the effect your attitudes have on your life.

Are you proactive, not allowing yourself to be manipulated into reacting to a situation? If you are not proactive, begin to practice taking a step back from a situation as it is happening. Reserve judgment until you silently count to 10 as you decide if your immediate reaction will serve you well. Does your attitude about the situation allow you not to jump to conclusions and to consider consequences prior to responding?

Have you broadened your thinking to finally realize that everyone is different and has an opinion; that there are no right or wrong answers, just different ways of doing anything? Everyone has a right to his or her own feelings. All feelings are valid!

What distinguishes us as individuals is our perspective on situations, our attitudes about life. Once you learn to respect the right of others to think differently than you do, you will have reached maturity.

Once you accept the fact that all people are unique, you can begin to focus on your needs. You can begin to protect your energy and honor the right of others to do the same. It is okay to feel insecure; each of us is insecure in some way. You are more likely to be respected when you respect yourself and exude it. LIFE IS NOT A CONTEST! Feel free to be who you are, not what someone else thinks you should be.

Accept responsibility for your own life, the good, the bad, the everything. Shape your thinking to eliminate the concept of blame. Life is not about blame; it is about understanding, accepting, respecting and appreciating. Don't blame others for what happens in your life. Try to accept things as they are; understand that you are no better nor worse than anyone else. What categorizes people is their opportunities and how they deal with those opportunities. Healthy attitudes can shape the opportunities that come your way and allow you to create your own opportunities.

Blaming steals precious energy and wastes time. Direct your life by adjusting your attitudes. You are a unique, complicated individual. Applaud your right to be different while appreciating others' rights to be who they are. Adjusting your attitudes frees you to be productive, allowing more energy to flow into your business. Feeling the need to constantly please others can also rob you of the energy you need to be productive. Accept that you can only change yourself.

Changing takes considerable effort. Every day, practice sending yourself messages about the attitudes you want to change. Remain in the present; picture yourself behaving differently than you do ordinarily. After about a month of these exercises (done daily), you will not have to work at it so hard, as it will become a natural part of your behavior pattern. The important thing to remember is to stop before you respond and to take responsibility for your thoughts, feelings and actions. By remaining in the conscious state when thinking about situations and your response to them, you can begin to change forever how you deal with others and the thought processes that can empower you to greater control over your life.

One way of shifting toward a more confident, more positive attitude is the approach of many first-time business owners: Fake it 'til you make it! You may not always feel confident inside, but if you can project confidence to others, the confidence will eventually sink into your being and become yours.

In Control vs. Controlling

Having a positive attitude helps you be in control of your feelings and actions—of who you are, what you say and what you do. Maintaining control will be essential in setting the standards and guiding principles by which you operate. While it's impossible to be in control every single moment, it will help you be more effective in generating revenues for your business.

Being in control is not about being "controlling," a negative term implying that you try to control and manipulate other people. What it's about is being aware of what's going on and remaining confident as to who you are. It's about controlling situations—getting what you need—without hurting anyone in the process. All people have their own attitudes, values and standards. You are not responsible for or in control of theirs, nor they yours. When you respect the right of all people to make their own choices, you'll be able to work toward outcomes in which both parties win. You can maintain control over your own life and destiny—you must, to be successful—without interfering with other people's control over themselves.

Being in control is not about being controlling

Maintaining control is actually a wonderful state of mind. It means that, understanding the values and guiding principles by which you live, you try hard to please yourself and achieve your personal standards, not those of other people. It means not allowing yourself to be unduly influenced by others, and it means being responsible for your own actions. Say to yourself, "If it is to be, it is up to me." Let these 10 little two-letter words be your mantra—they are extremely powerful. Recite them when you need a boost, when you awaken in the morning, before bed at night—every chance you get! Say them, listen to them and take in what they mean. They will reassure you that you have the power.

Protecting Your Energy

Energy is the driving force of everything, living or mechanical. Your energy is a precious asset that requires—even deserves—protection. You need it to stay focused on running a profitable business.

Protecting your energy means having control over your conscious thoughts. It means accepting the responsibility for protecting yourself from those who may try to manipulate you and from people or situations that diminish your confidence or self-esteem. It means not allowing people—associates, family, employees, clients, whomever—to pull you down and zap your energy. Negative people in general, especially those who whine or complain all the time, will drain your energy just as quickly. Listening to or being with someone who requires a lot of attention is also draining.

Gain control over the ebb and flow of your energy by being conscious of your feelings as you experience them. When you know you are depleted, protect your energy by deferring discussions or decisions. You'll make better decisions when your energy levels are normal or high. "Now is not a good time." "May we do this another time?" and "I need to go; I will get back to you," are all ways to defer conversations or decisions. Don't hesitate to use them.

Dealing With Anger

Anger can be tremendously debilitating, stripping your energy and severely diminishing your productivity for entire days or more. Often, the people you're angry with will never even know of your anger (especially if you don't tell them), it doesn't impact them at all. The point is: being angry hurts you. By remaining calm—by not reacting and not becoming angry—you conserve and protect your energy. In this way, anger and residual bad feelings won't constrict you, allowing you to move on mentally and to maintain your productivity.

Results of a study on anger conducted by Duke University revealed that people who are angry on a regular basis:

- Consume an additional 600 calories per day than those not angry,

- Tend to die six years sooner than others their same age/height/weight,

- Make more frequent trips to doctors' offices with medical complaints,

- Have a greater incidence of high blood pressure and blood clots.

To deal effectively with anger, you need to understand why you become angry under certain circumstances. The next exercise gives you the opportunity to understand and recognize when anger is occurring and to examine how you deal with it. On a separate piece of paper, complete each of the following sentences:

1. **I become angry when . . .**

2. **When I become angry, I . . .**

3. **When someone becomes angry with me, I . . .**

4. **I reduce my angry feelings by . . .**

5. **I find it easiest to become angry (when, about) . . .**

Anger is born of fear, generally because you fear losing something to or being jeopardized by another person. For example, if you respond with anger to someone suddenly swerving into your lane while driving, the anger might come from fear of being injured or killed. Or, maybe you fear being late to an appointment.

Examine each of your responses to the above exercise and begin to probe why you react that way. Ask yourself, "What is it that I fear?" and "Why am I reacting or responding to a particular situation with anger?"

Getting in touch with the fear helps you to be more proactive, as opposed to reactive. It allows you to be more in control of your anger and of the situation. To succeed in running a business, to influence people and to generate consistent business revenue, it is important to be proactive. Stop, think and strategize how to respond in a positive way rather than simply reacting to a given situation.

Taking responsibility for your feelings, your actions and for who you are is another way to control your anger. It makes you stop and think before reacting. You cannot always change situations, but you can always change how you feel about situations.

Having A Vision

Working with thousands of microbusiness owners over the years has made me aware of the necessity of having a vision. Rarely will microbusiness owners succeed unless they have a clear vision of what they hope to accomplish. Being visionary takes guts and courage, for with vision comes criticism. No one can see with your eyes and mind, so others will resent your ability to focus on what you want. Dare to have a dream of a special future, a business, a lifestyle. Don't allow others to quash your dreams because they cannot see your vision and don't understand it. Know that you are an individual with all the rights and privileges accorded an occupant of the universe.

> **"...as we let our own light shine, we consciously give other people permission to do the same."**

In his inaugural speech, Nelson Mandela said, "Our deepest fear is not that we are inadequate. Our deepest fear is that we are powerful beyond measure. It is our light, not darkness, that most frightens us. We ask ourselves: Who am I to be brilliant, gorgeous, talented and fabulous? Actually...who are you not to be? You are a child of God. Your playing small doesn't serve the world. There is nothing enlightened about shrinking so that other people won't feel insecure around you. We were born to make manifest the glory of God that is within us. It's not just in some of us, it's in everyone. As we let our own light shine, we consciously give other people permission to do the same. As we are liberated from our own fear, our presence automatically liberates others."

Recognize the fear of success and work on becoming liberated from it so that your light can shine. In order to achieve success in a business, a plan is needed, and the engine of that plan is a vision. Without a driving force, your plan would have no energy to move forward. Allow yourself to envision where you will be 5, 10 and 20 years from now. Try this simple creative-visualization exercise: Find a quiet area where you will be uninterrupted for at least 10 minutes. Sit in a relaxed position, with head back and feet elevated, if possible. Play soft music in the background to set the mood.

Begin by closing your eyes and seeing yourself in the future.

- What will you look like two years from now?
- How hard will you work?
- How will your business be managed?
- How much money will you make?
- Are you being proactive rather than reactive?
- What will be the hook that causes consumers to patronize your business?
- What will you do in your spare time?
- Who will help you with the business?
- How large is the area (office, showroom, etc.) where you work?
- How much time do you spend doing the things you enjoy outside of work?

When coming out of the visualization, move slowly back to the present, seeing as you return the changes you will make in the future. If you can get in the habit of visualizing, you will notice your capacity to produce will increase, allowing you to complete more tasks in an efficient manner.

Here is another exercise to demonstrate the power of having a vision: Stand with your feet apart, making sure there is room for you to swing your extended arms in either direction without moving your feet. Allow yourself a moment to just relax, and then, without moving your feet and only using your body from the hips up, extend an arm (the one used to write) and twist your body in the direction of that arm as far as you can. Hold the position and make a mental note of how far you were able to go; then return to the first position with arms along your side.

Relax again, and shake your body to stimulate it. Close your eyes and visualize yourself going much farther than the first time. Reassure yourself that you can go farther. After a moment, assume the stance and complete the journey again. Notice how much farther you are able to go this time. I have watched count-less individuals do this exercise and never has someone failed to go farther the second time after having envisioned themselves doing just that.

PROCEED WITH CAUTION

The power of the mind is beyond imagination. Being visionary increases your ability to use your brain to a higher degree than is usual.

NOTE: As you work to develop yourself, it is helpful to read a daily inspirational passage from any number of available books. Some provide a day-by-day message on a specific topic. There are religious books. There are books designed for specific ethnic groups. Eric V. Copage's Black Pearls for African-Americans is a good source, as is Tony Robbins. Such passages make you stop and think, even if just for a moment.

Try to devote at least 15 minutes every morning—make it a part of your daily routine—to reading or writing in a journal. Or, just use the time to reflect on things you've done or are working toward. This is the time to work on you. I often do it while still in bed, just before I get up. I visualize my day, read an inspiration or affirmation, then it's up and at 'em with renewed vigor. This kind of inner work helps you improve your attitude and your ability to take charge of your life, make better decisions, protect your energy, and be a better person.

CHAPTER TWO

Are You Up to the Challenge?

Commitment—The "C" Word

Starting a microbusiness of any kind is challenging and requires a high degree of commitment. If you're already in business, you understand exactly what I mean. Don't take this "C word" lightly!

Commitment to making a business work often means that your friends and family don't get as much of your time as you once gave them. It means working more than 40 hours a week to make the business really happen, more like 60 to 80 hours weekly. Often sacrifice is the order of the day, week, month and year. You may have to renegotiate relationships, abstain from pleasures and refrain from buying material things such as a new car or home.

Commitment means taking the time to learn the different tasks you'll need to complete to make the business work. People often start businesses with a particular skill or expertise but without the experience or requisite skills to run an effective business. These include, but are not limited to: marketing effectively, keeping records, understanding finance, completing administrative tasks and being the "gofer" for whatever needs doing. Commitment also means assuming responsibility for all the tasks of operating a business. And it means remaining open and adaptable so that you can make the adjustments that will lead to your success.

Go into business with your eyes open, conscious of the commitment required. This way you will prepare yourself, as well as those around you, for putting a majority of your energy into operating your business. If you're unwilling to make this commitment, think twice about starting a business. The statistics are not in your favor; chances of success are very slim. Even if all you want is a part-time business to operate in your spare time for a little extra cash, you still need a strong commitment, probably greater than you anticipate, to give that business a chance to succeed.

The Five "Ds" of Successful Microbusiness Ownership

Following are the five distinct qualities of a successful entrepreneur.

DESIRE. Desire is the carrot that dangles in front of you, the vision that burns in the heart of every business owner. If your desire to be an entrepreneur is strong enough, it will point you toward success and provide the fuel to get you there.

DILIGENCE. Diligence is persistently and attentively making the most of your opportunities and options. It means developing your strength and overcoming any lack of skill, education, space or money. You learn what you need to and do what you must to get the job done.

DETAIL-MINDED. Being detail-minded is a special skill of most successful entrepreneurs, who are usually supreme organizers. Some use a simple "To Do" list on their desks. Others employ a battery of computers and organizational schemes. While these ways of dealing with the details differ, you will never find a truly successful entrepreneur without a well-oiled organizational system.

DISCIPLINE. Discipline is a sister to detail and diligence because it is hard to have one without the other. One of the nation's most successful salesmen attributes his success to doing the things that other salesmen don't want to do—the things that are difficult or uncomfortable or that require sacrifice. Your success requires that you discipline yourself to accomplish those tasks you would rather put off or avoid altogether.

DETERMINATION. Determination is closely related to desire and diligence but is more than the two combined. It's what keeps you going when the going gets tough. It is the measure of your character. It means seeing your dreams through to completion.

If one has these five qualities, it's difficult to be anything but proactive and positive. They also go a long way toward raising your confidence level. How do you rate with each of the five? Is there a "D" that you're weaker in (such as "discipline")? What can you do to improve it?

Risk Taking

There is not an entrepreneur alive who has made a business work without taking some amount of risk. Running a business is risky by nature. To be successful, you'll wind up taking more risks than many others. So be sure to think through your risks. Research and understand all of the consequences of a risk. Know what you're getting into. Weigh the pros and cons to determine whether you really should take the risk.

Consider the following when evaluating your risks, being realistic about the depth of the risk:

- **What is the worst that can happen to you?**

- **Will it kill you?**

- **Will it seriously hurt anyone?**

- **Will you be able to walk away from your business and investment, if necessary?**

- **Will you regret not having done it?**

- **Are you dealing with a calculated risk or a gamble?**

EXAMPLE: *Your initial financial projections indicate that to make the business work, you will need $25,000, yet you have only $3,000. You decide to chance it in hopes that you generate enough revenue to make up the difference. This is a gamble, plain and simple. There is little chance, if any, that you can make it happen. The numbers are just not there. You're destined to join the 90 percent of businesses that fail. Not even bothering to do the financial projections would have made it an even worse gamble.*

As in other aspects of your business (and life), it helps to have a process for determining whether to take a particular risk. It could be a process as simplistic as Ben Franklin's old technique of weighing the pros and cons: Make two parallel columns down a sheet of paper, listing the pros in one column and the cons in the other. Which column has more entries? How will the exercise affect what you do?

Some tips for risk taking:

- **Hedge your bets. Find whatever cushion you can that will make the risk less consequential.**

- **Anticipate alternative solutions. Is there more than one way to do this? Which is the lesser of two evils or the road of less resistance?**

- **Always have a backup plan. If you do this and it doesn't work, what will you do? How can you still manage to complete your mission? Can you take longer to achieve your objectives? Can you do only a small part of the plan?**

Decision Making

To run an effective business, it's important to have a process for making decisions about anything, whether it involves risk or not. It is unwise to make decisions based solely on emotions; you are likely to regret such decisions. Be objective when evaluating a situation. Make decisions based on information and understanding of the variables.

This seven-step approach will help.

1. State the situation. If it involves solving a problem, define the problem and what caused it. Quantify it if possible; how many times has this happened and for how long? What is the likelihood of recurrence?

2. Define the objectives. What action must be taken to deal with the situation or resolve the problem?

3. Develop a diagnostic framework. What methods will you use? What information do you need?

4. Collect and analyze the necessary information. Gather charts, data, indexes, records, etc., and investigate them. Are there any patterns or trends?

5. Determine alternative solutions and their consequences. What if this, what if that, what if? Rank the solutions in order of feasibility.

6. Develop an action plan. Base it on your analysis of information. Once you decide on a plan, implement it. You'll get no results if you don't implement it!

CAUTION

**SLIPPERY
WHEN WET**

7. Obtain and evaluate feedback on what you have done. This helps you to know whether you've made a good decision. If you didn't, start the process over to reach a different, more viable result.

Developing a thorough, automatic decision-making process will greatly enhance your success in business—and in life! It will help you preserve valuable energy, as well. The key is to develop a system to which you can, and will, stick.

EXAMPLE: *you are trying to decide whether to start a business. You have a good-paying job but you are not happy, you have always wanted to have your own business and you are not getting any younger. You have considered several businesses but have not determined which one to develop. The decision is two-fold: should you quit a good-paying job and start a business, and what business do you start?*

To use the seven-step approach in this situation, you should:

1. Explore the situation. Determine how long you have wanted to start a business. Do you want to start a business because you don't like your job, or are you really hankering to run your own business? How badly do you want a business?

2. Have a frank discussion with yourself to see whether you understand what it takes to run a business effectively. Possibly, determine what outcomes you would like to see occur. Clearly identify what the options are, then figure out what steps you should take to explore them.

3. Determine the techniques you will use to identify and explore these options. Try a pro-and-con evaluation of the options, or research what you stand to gain by choosing either option. Determine what information you will need to examine so that your research will be thorough.

4. Do the necessary research. Look for patterns in your behavior that indicate whether you have the tenacity to operate a business. Explore what it takes to run each potential business, then determine which, if either, business will be the best option.

5. Decide what you would do if you chose a business and decided later that you weren't happy with it. If you could stay on the job and retire with a pension or profit sharing settlement, would you still want to start a business? What

other alternatives exist if you choose not to start a business at this time? Explore all options. Rank the conclusions in order of their feasibility.

6. Decide what action you must take on your choice. (In this example, where so much is at stake and so much needs to be done to make it happen, get feedback from others and evaluate prior to actually implementing.)

7. Assess your decision and move forward if it proves to be feasible and comfortable. If not, be still; don't make any changes until you rethink the process.

CHAPTER THREE

Communicating Your Way to Success

Communication is the key to success or failure. If you can communicate effectively with people, you can be successful running a business. Good communication skills make you able to negotiate better deals, be more effective in sales and increase your profits. By becoming more aware of your own communication patterns and those of others, you can increase your success and satisfaction in business and in life. Once you're aware of established patterns, changing them requires flexibility, a strong ability to overcome resistance and a steadfast belief system. Sound like a tall order? It does require dedication and effort. But the rewards are worth it. This chapter will help put you on the road to more successful communication.

To communicate effectively with other people, you must learn how to:

- **Ask for what you want**
- **Build rapport**
- **Take charge of a situation**
- **Change your own response to create change in others**
- **Interpret the dynamics of power in relationships.**

How to Ask

Years ago, motivational speaker and author Tony Robbins developed five key points to asking that have greatly assisted me in getting what I've needed over the years. Practice these points every time you ask for something. You'll be surprised to notice how much more effective you can become at getting what you want.

1. Know what you want. You can't get what you want if you don't know what it is—specifically. Don't even begin to ask for something until your request is clear in your mind. It may help to write it down, refining it until you know exactly what you want. Then, be sure to actually ask the question—don't fall into the trap of expecting someone to read your mind. Couples do this all the time: get irritated because they don't get what they want, when they never even verbalized what that was. Know what you want and ask for it before you expect someone to give it to you.

> ...don't fall into the trap of expecting someone to read your mind.

2. Ask someone who can give it to you. Many people make the mistake of expecting others to give them something that the person may be incapable of giving. For example, you wouldn't expect a baby to be able to hand you a 30-pound weight. Nor would you ask a homeless person to give you $50. But the issue relates to more than just money or material items. It deals with emotional giving as well. We often expect the people with whom we are involved emotionally to be different than they really are. You may need your mate to verbally express his or her feelings, when doing so is not within his or her ability, for whatever reason. Before you ask for something, decide whether the person actually has the ability to give you what you request. It is often difficult to know another's capacity to give. Indeed, this is the most challenging point of asking.

3. Have a congruent belief that you will get what you want. If you don't believe it, you can't expect anyone else to believe it either. This is about attitude and about choosing your words carefully. Imagine calling and asking someone, "Maybe you could, uh, do you think you possibly might?" No! This uncertain tone will get you nowhere. Practice asking more confidently in front of a mirror, speak into a tape recorder, write a script for your question. Face yourself, listen to the words you choose, ask yourself whether you believe, whether you sound confident. The more confident you appear and sound, the more likely you are to get what you request, as long as the person has the power to give it to you.

4. **Build value for the person you are asking.** It is important to make the person you are asking feel that giving you what you want is of some value to them. As children, we all knew that we were more likely to win favors from our parents if we did our chores first. It still works the same way: Make the person feel good, and he or she is more likely to give you what you want. Building value doesn't have to mean that you give something of equal value. It may simply mean that you express appreciation, show sincerity or impress upon who you ask the critical nature of your need and what a fantastic service that person would be providing. Take the time to think about what you could say or do to make that person want to help you.

5. **Ask until!** Persistence is the name of the game. If you don't receive what you need from the first person you ask, try someone else. In fact, ask the first person to refer you to someone who can help you. Assess the ability of others to give you what you want and keep asking. Don't feel reject-ed—understand that there are many reasons why people respond the way they do. Most often, a negative response has nothing to do with you as a person, so don't take it per-sonally. Perhaps the person didn't understand or wasn't capable of giving. Don't give up either—just keep asking! Many great business people had to ask hundreds of times before getting what they wanted. Col. Sanders of Kentucky Fried Chicken tried to sell his recipe for chicken to more than a hundred companies before he found the money to start his own business. Fred Smith of Federal Express faced repossession of his leased planes but kept asking until he got enough help to land his company on solid ground. Ask until you get what you want!

Knowing how to ask gives you immense power and effectiveness in your business. It certainly has paid off for me, as the follow-ing anecdotes will show you. In June 1995, I started the Women's Business Training Center. Being a nonprofit organiza-tion, we didn't have a lot of money to get off the ground. When officers of a local bank whom we had invited to participate on our board asked how they could help, I immediately responded that we needed office space and offered to use the bank's name and logo on the Center's materials. The bank had the ability to help and received value (good public relations from funding a community service project) for doing so. The bank readily agreed to donate space for the Center.

Another is that I was allowed to participate for free in a special program that would normally have cost me $300 to $400 a

Take the time to think about what you could say or do to make that person want to help you.

month. I asked very humbly for the privilege and gave evidence as to how it would benefit not only me but the company sponsoring the program. I became the only person in the country to be granted that privilege. In fact, in almost every instance throughout my life that I put this technique to use, I've received what I requested.

Building Rapport

Effectiveness in communication relies on establishing rapport, a relationship of mutual trust. Rapport is the state of likeness, verbally or nonverbally. The underlying concept in building rapport is that when people identify with you, they are more likely to cooperate with you. That's because we tend to feel more comfortable with people who are more like us. Building rapport, then, is the best way to overcome any resistance to what you want in a situation.

...we tend to feel more comfortable with people who are more like us.

Notice how often you say you like someone after hearing her or him say things you agree with or in which you believe. And you'll often dislike people who constantly challenge or put down your perspective. What you're really saying is, "They aren't like me. I don't feel comfortable around them." Be conscious of the things you have in common with people.

Emphasize your similarities rather than your differences. When you build that level of comfort for the other person, you consciously take charge of the situation and attract cooperation.

Taking Charge of a Situation

One of the realities of effective communication is this: Either you control the situation or it controls you. To understand how to take control, you must first determine what is the prevailing reality—what you are trying to accomplish and what the other person understands or believes about what is happening. Then you must align yourself with the other person's reality, working with rather than against that person. Be aware of what that person deems to be reality. Probe to discover what that person's feelings are (his or her reality) about the subject at hand. The information will enable you to make the person feel comfortable, thus permitting you to ease into the driver's seat.

Some people are uncomfortable with the notion of controlling a situation. Understand that this is not a contest of will or strength. Nor is it about manipulation or control in any negative sense. Think of it more as guiding or directing the flow of conversation and events. Doing so keeps attention focused on the issue and gently pushes everyone toward decisions, resolutions and conclusions. Everyone's needs get considered. Controlling the situation allows for a win-win situation.

How do we begin to control conversations or situations? Start by being more of a listener than a talker. People love to talk about themselves, about their businesses. But it's the listener who actually controls the situation. That's because the person who is talking is not learning. Information is only flowing out, not in. Well-timed questions and statements keep the other person talking and help guide the conversation.

Cybernetics, the study of automated control systems in both humans and machines, offers more lessons for controlling situations. One fascinating tenet is the Law of Requisite Variety, which simply means that the individual (or machine) with the widest range of responses will control the situation, all other factors being equal. For example, if you have more variety in your sales pitch than the person resisting your pitch, you should be able to control the outcome. Keep in mind that we are talking about win-win situations in which you are not taking unfair advantage of or manipulating individuals.

Another strategy for taking charge of a situation is pacing. Basically, it means meeting other people at their level and reflecting what they know, see or assume to be true. It means matching some part of their experience. For example, in a conversation with a soft-spoken woman, you would speak in a soft tone. If she moves forward to listen more intently, you do the same. (Remember, listeners usually control the circumstances!)

There are various ways to pace. You can pace a person's mood, body language and speech patterns (including rate of speech, tonality or volume). You can pace a person's beliefs and opinions by saying, "I agree with that," or "I feel the same way." Emulating a person's breathing pattern, taking deep breaths or being out of breath, also allows you to pace them. The wider your range of understanding and human experience, the easier it is to pace a variety of personality types and behaviors.

Pacing is a natural response and something that we do on a regular basis without always being consciously aware of it. You're better off, however, doing it consciously. Being aware of what's going on in situations is the only way you can hope to control them and get what you want. Being aware also can help you detect how others might be pacing you. I call it leveling the playing field. Remember, either you control the situation or it controls you!

Effective communication also hinges on establishing trust and credibility with the other person. The trust and credibility comes when people begin to feel comfortable with you and rapport is established. If this isn't happening, you must work at being a good listener, being more expressive and being sensitive of others' circumstances.

Achieving these skills will go a long way toward establishing trust and credibility with the other person. To do this, you must be aware of your effectiveness. You must feel confident in your ability to win friends and influence people. You must be flexible so that you can change the patterns that you use and be able to pace people effectively. You must have a strong ability to overcome resistance. Be steadfast in your belief system. Be steadfast in your ability to be flexible and be in the present, consciously aware of what is going on around you.

Changing How You Respond

To communicate persuasively, you need to have a system by which you operate—a dynamic and changeable system, such that a shift in one part prompts change in other parts, re-establishing equilibrium. A system is a process used to handle a particular circumstance. The system is your principles and the standards that guide you. Trust them and live up to them, and chances are you'll make good decisions.

The underlying assumption here is that you can't change other people, but you can change how you deal with and respond to them. So, as you change and readjust, the other person must make adjustments to keep the balance. The question is always: What specific change must you make to provoke the desired change in someone else? It often requires lots of contemplation.

From the time she was very young, I tried to get my daughter to understand that she had the power not to let others dictate her moods or how she responded to situations. I deliberately said things to annoy her, then encouraged her to understand that she could choose to ignore those things and not allow them to upset her. I was trying to instill in her a simple principle: she may choose how to respond.

> **...you can't change other people, but you can change how you deal with and respond to them.**

Now an attorney, she recently said to me, "Even though I never liked it when you did that to me, I understand now what you were trying to accomplish, and I'm grateful." She knows now that she has power and control over her own life, and she chooses how she will respond to people.

People often tell me that they don't understand how I remain calm in trying circumstances. "It comes from learning over the years," I say to them, "to choose my reactions to people and situations." When people say or do things that annoy or irritate me, I distance myself from them and from the situation, rather than give it credibility by reacting. This disarms and diffuses the whole situation. When people do not get the desired response to their actions, they will often stop doing it because the action no longer works. Not getting the desired response throws everything off.

Practice being in control of your situation. Practice at home with loved ones, at the office and in your dealings with business people. Hone your people skills to become more effective in getting what you want for yourself and your business. You may not be able to control what someone says to you, but you can always control how you are affected by what they say and how you respond. It's all a matter of choice and being proactive.

Relationships and Power

Relationships are the cornerstones on which you build an operation. Without relationships, you would fail to operate a successful, profitable business—indeed, there would be no business! Relationships exist with many types of people in business: suppliers, customers or clients, subcontractors, and employees.

It's important to recognize that with every one of these relationships, there will be some form of power struggle—consciously or unconsciously—as to who will be in control in that relationship. For there to be a healthy balance in relationships, power must be shared. Sometimes, depending on the personalities involved, this doesn't happen. Some people insist on having all the power. Do what you must to protect your power and not allow anyone to take it from you.

For example, you are obligated to make clients or customers think they are always right, even when you know they are not. Sharing power allows the customer or client to feel they are respected and encourages them to continue as customers or clients.

Insecure people too easily relinquish their power.

Insecure people too easily relinquish their power. Consequently, they feel less in control of their lives and of what happens to them. Recognizing the dynamics of power in relationships is the first step. Take baby steps. Set out each day to have a small victory: Let someone know they have offended you, do something to communicate your true feelings and to stick up for yourself.

Map the steps to slowly gain confidence and dignity. Plan your work, and then work your plan. If you falter, quickly get back in step and keep going. As it is in so many aspects of business, setting goals—and the objectives necessary to make them happen—is a critical part of this effort.

Making SMART Goals

Goal setting is the single most powerful tool for use in operating your business, bar none! Learning how to use this tool will increase your odds of achieving success and sustaining a profitable business for many years.

As previously discussed, the only way to be in control of your business, your life or any situation is to have a vision. Without vision, you may be able to go along day to day, but you'll never rise above a survival mode. For goals to be meaningful and achievable, you must be able to envision them. At stake is whether your business flies or just sits on the ground because of a lack of vision.

For some people, goal setting is very unnerving. They may feel uncomfortable making commitments even for a few hours away. This is especially true for those suffering from attention deficit disorder (ADD) or attention deficit-hyperactive disorder (ADHD). Other maladies cause similar anxiety about being too structured. And some people are just not comfortable planning ahead.

Although goal setting can be difficult for many of us, there are strategies to facilitate getting on track and focusing. Start by focusing on tasks rather than goals. Become task-oriented. If writing a plan makes you nervous, then map out strategies for your success. Lastly, take small steps toward outlining the tasks to complete. Sneak up on the idea of doing tasks everyday that will lead you to an accomplishment.

A Harvard University study in the 1970s indicated that only 13 percent of the population sets goals. If you're not a goal setter, you're in the majority. But the majority of people also fail in business! To be in the minority that is successful, you must also be in the minority of those who set goals.

Setting goals—SMART goals—will change your life. It will give you power and control over your business and other aspects of your life. It will give you a significantly better chance of achieving success and profits. It will allow you to actually run your business, rather than letting it run you.

That was the widely popular title of a business advice column I once wrote: "Are You Running Your Business or Is It Running You?" What it asks is whether you are so busy trying to keep up with your business that you end up behind, chasing it, rather than in front, leading it. If you have not set goals, you probably are playing catch up. The business is running you—perhaps even running over you!

A recent client who had been in business for seven years is a good example of this. She produces a wonderful product that is well-received by all those who see it. She came to me saying she had completely lost control of her business. She knew she had to regain control or lose the business. When I asked what her gross profits were the previous year, her response was, "I don't know." She responded the same when I asked about her average sales. The client explained to me that she didn't like numbers and was not a very good record keeper. She knew that money was coming in, but she couldn't account for where it was going.

After close examination, we discovered that she had generated more than $100,000 in revenues the previous year. She had no idea that her income was so high! We also discovered that she probably could have made an additional $18,000 without selling additional products. To do so, however, she had to be in control of her business. It took more than seven months, but she finally gained control. She knows what it takes to make the business operate. She has charted a course for her business, developing goals that make sense and are achievable. She even plans to expand the business within a year, probably doubling revenue and more than doubling the number of employees/contractors with whom she works.

The only way this client could achieve such control—control that greatly affects her money-making ability—was by setting goals and knowing what it takes to be in control of her operation. She began to look at her business in a totally different manner. No longer is she afraid of numbers; she takes the time to be meticulous about keeping records and looks at the numbers to understand how to make them work for her. She has control over the direction in which the business is headed. SMART goal setting saved her business.

SMART is a goal-setting model that over the years I've adapted to my approach to business development. Using this model will help you set goals to achieve your vision and be in control of your business. SMART goal setting is:

- **S**pecific
- **M**anageable and Measurable
- **A**ttainable
- **R**ealistic
- **T**ime-sensitive

"S" is for SPECIFIC

Let's start with a quiz. Which of the following are SMART goals?

- To raise money to start a business
- To lose weight
- To increase your clientele

None of them is. That's because none of the goals is clear and specific, the first requirement in SMART goal setting. We set ourselves up to fail by making goals that are not clear and specific—and therefore achievable. Then, when we do fail, we beat up on ourselves and start a vicious cycle that can be broken by setting SMART goals.

Try putting each of the above goals in more specific language. Here are some examples:

- To raise $7,000 to start a business by October 1 of next year
- To lose 100 pounds in a year
- To attract six more solid clients by year-end

These are starting to be clearer and more specific. Goals should be quantifiable, if possible ($7,000; 100 pounds; six clients).

"M" is for **MANAGEABLE** and **MEASURABLE**

The thought of raising $7,000 to start a business by October 1 of next year might be a bit overwhelming. To make it more palatable, break it down into manageable segments. If October 1 is 14 months away, we could divide the $7,000 into segments of $500 a month. This breaks down into only $125 a week, making the entire goal seem far more achievable.

But we're not done yet. We need to measure our progress in putting together the $7,000. Having broken our $7,000 goal down into manageable segments, we can use a simple calendar approach to figure out where we are in the process of accumulating $500 a month for 14 months. We sum up our totals monthly or bi-monthly and examine the result. If, for example, we don't have $1,000 after two months, we may have to reevaluate whether we are on the right track. Is the action plan we developed to achieve this goal working for us? Is our goal still something we can achieve? Do we need to adjust our plan?

Flexibility—the ability to make necessary adjustments—is a critical ingredient in SMART goal setting. Perhaps, using our current example, we need to lower the amount we are trying to raise. Perhaps we need to brainstorm other sources of revenue. Would getting a part-time job enable us to stick to our $500 a month plan?

Measuring where you are at regular intervals keeps you in control of your goal, allowing you to make decisions based on information, rather than guessing. Without knowing where you are in a process, you can't make adjustments; you won't even know you need adjustments.

"A" is for **ATTAINABLE**

Attainability measures your ability or capacity to achieve your goal. Examine your capacity in three areas:

1. Financial
2. Physical
3. Emotional

Are you capable of achieving this goal in each of these three areas? Financially, can you afford to put aside $125 a week? Do you have the physical capability, whatever is required, to generate $125 a week? Are you emotionally ready to make the commitment to find an extra $125 a week, however it is that you come by it? Your answer to each question must be "yes" throughout the time you have set to achieve the goal.

If you are unable to say "yes", you must reassess. Either adjust the goal or decide that the goal is not something you can achieve now. It's critical to assess your capability for achieving a goal at various intervals throughout the process. Discovering after 14 months that your $7,000 goal was unattainable means you wasted valuable time and energy. Failing to meet your goal often produces a loss of self-confidence. So make sure you're ready and able before attempting a goal. Since circumstances can change at anytime—be prepared to suspend a goal if you become incapable of achieving it. Be aware of changes and be ready to assess your capability at any given time.

"R" is for REALISTIC

How realistic is it for you to think that you can raise $7,000 in 14 months? If you are on unemployment or have no income, it certainly would not be realistic to expect that you could do so. You probably wouldn't have the financial capability of doing it even if you had the physical and emotional capability. Or, if an emergency arose, how realistic is it that you could continue to accumulate $7,000 over a 14-month period?

At any given time during the course of achieving the goal, you must be able to know that it is realistic and achievable. If it is not, then you must stop the process.

"T" is for TIME-SENSITIVE

SMART goals are time-sensitive. They don't go on indefinitely; they have a deadline or a time frame. That time frame provides motivation to complete the goal. Without a time frame, there is no use even setting goals, for a timeless goal will never be achieved.

Learning to set goals and achieve them is a talent. You must first realize that goal setting is nothing more than:

- Knowing where you want to go,
- Predicting the probability of getting there,
- Researching which paths will lead to desired outcomes,
- Monitoring your progress.

Personal Goals

In the holistic approach to business development, setting personal goals is just as important as setting goals for your business. If you spend all your time and energy focusing on your business goals—to the exclusion of personal goals—your life will be out of balance. Allow yourself the opportunity and the right to have personal goals, and take the time to apply the SMART goal-setting model to those goals. Merge your personal goals with your business goals.

EXAMPLE: *Imagine that you want to take vacation three weeks out of every year, and you want the business to be in a position to pay for those vacations. Several things need to happen. First, the business needs to generate enough revenue to cover the cost of the vacation. Second, you must have someone whom you trust and who is capable of running the business to fill in for you while you're gone. You also must feel worthy of taking that vacation.*

If you are married, the personal goals of your spouse come into play as well. For example, if your spouse is set on you both retiring in 10 years, your goal must reflect that. How do you prepare the business for your retirement, while allowing it to continue after that time? Goal setting will help you work through all the implications of such a move and all the steps you need to take to make it happen.

The Action Plan

Every goal requires an action plan, a written strategy for accomplishing the goal. Consider it a map to find the treasure that achieving the goal will yield. Without one, goal setting is likely to be futile. The process involves breaking down each goal into objectives, or the tasks needed to accomplish the goal. Objectives then become mini-goals that also need timelines for completion. Break these objectives down into manageable, measurable segments and they become items on your daily "To Do" list.

Let's use our previous example. How are you going to get the $125 a week it will take to raise $7,000 in 14 months to start a business? (Note that it probably won't be exactly $125 every week; some weeks may bring in more than others.) Here are some objectives you might include in an action plan. Under each objective are steps that would begin to constitute a "To Do" list.

WEEK ONE: Examine household budget to see where expenses can be cut.
- Organize receipts by month.
- Divide expenses for previous month into categories.
- Tally all expense receipts by category; place on spreadsheet.
- Examine totals; decide how much to cut from each expense category monthly.
- Put aside stock dividends received the first week of every month.
- Open bank account for business fund by week four.
- Arrange for direct deposit of dividend check within first month.

What are other steps the person in this example might include in an action plan? Take some time here to make a list. Put the list away for a day, and see if you can brainstorm some more ideas. Be as creative—but realistic—as you can.

Here are some tried-and-true tips for goal setting and action plans:

BREAK IT DOWN. Break down the goal into the smallest, most manageable tasks to be accomplished, being specific about details.

WRITE IT DOWN. Written goals are much more likely to be accomplished than those that are not. But don't write them down and tuck them away. You'll lose sight of them—literally and figuratively. Place your lists where you can see them every day, or at least where you will review them regularly, be it weekly, monthly or quarterly. A good place is your appointment book.

START WITH SMALL STEPS. If you're not used to setting goals, begin by taking small steps that will gradually get you into the habit. Set goals that require only an hour or two to accomplish. Then start setting daily and weekly goals. As you start to see the value of SMART goal setting, you're likely to get hooked.

REWARD YOURSELF FOR SUCCESSES. Give yourself lots of credit for achieving goals, however small. Rewards can be as tangible as the pair of earrings that you've been coveting for months or a triple-dip ice cream cone. Perhaps a hot bath with candles will do it, or granting yourself a few hours off to ride your bike, whatever makes you feel rewarded.

NOW GO FOR LONGER GOALS. After you've gotten in the habit of setting daily and weekly goals, begin to set short and long-term goals for the company. Short-term goals are normally for two years or less; long-term goals, for more than two years. Map out your action plan just as you have for your smaller goals. Be sure to include a time frame. Now you're really ready for the vast benefits that come your way from goal setting.

Learning to effectively set goals and establish objectives will give you unprecedented control over your business and your life. You'll earn a larger income, be more productive, manage time more efficiently, and be better able to balance work and family or work and free time—these and so many other benefits. It's just natural: When you know how to get where you want to be, you become more successful!

The bottom line is that SMART goal setting is empowering. All you have to do is start. One never stumbles upon sustained success; it can only result from careful planning (goal setting). Plan your work and then work your plan.

SECTION II

● **PREPARING THE VEHICLE FOR THE TRIP**

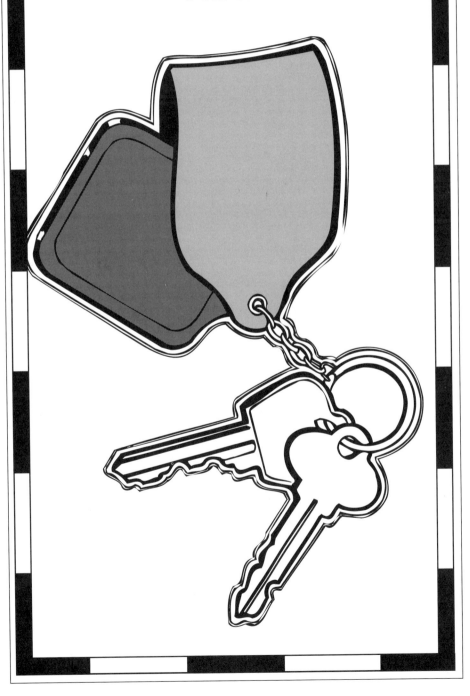

CHAPTER FIVE

Understanding Your Legal Rights and Responsibilities

Getting Legal—DBAs and Licenses

Once you decide to start a business, or if you currently operate one, you need to make it legal. Find out what the requirements are in your city, county or state. Whatever you do, don't shirk your duties here. If a government agency says you need a license to operate, get one. Penalties can be imposed if guidelines aren't followed. Additionally, if you inadvertently use someone else's name, there could be very costly consequences, including having to change all of your written materials, notifying clients or customers of a name change and the expense of changing phone listings and directories. You can avoid all this with a simple check of local records.

In most counties, you must register the name of your business by filing what is called a fictitious business statement, or DBA (doing business as). Changing or adding something to your name requires another filing. Find out which government office does registrations—it's often the county clerk's office. The registration process usually requires that you publish your DBA (normally in a newspaper) so that the general public knows who the business owner is and how to locate that person.

Also, most businesses must have a city business license. Certain types of businesses require special licenses to operate: liquor stores, beauty salons, restaurants or cafes, massage studios, construction companies and more. Chances are that if you're in one of those fields, you already know whether you need to be licensed. Be sure you understand exactly what you need for the particular kind of business you intend to operate.

There are presently four legal forms of business ownership: sole proprietorship, partnership, corporation and limited liability company (LLC). Below is a discussion of each, along with their respective benefits and drawbacks. Choosing the right form of ownership is important so that you don't pay unnecessary taxes.

Sole Proprietorships

The sole proprietor owns the business alone and, therefore, assumes all responsibility for that business. Some of the advantages of a sole proprietorship are:

- **It is easy to start.**

- **All profits are yours.**

- **One person makes the decisions.**

- **There are few government controls. Normally, all a sole proprietor needs to start is a DBA registration and a business license.**

The disadvantages of being a sole proprietor are:

Unlimited liability. If you are sued, everything you own can be attached: stocks, bonds, real estate, cars, jewelry.

Loans are difficult to acquire. Banks are leery of lending to a sole proprietor because if something happens to that person, there is no guarantee the bank would get its money back, even with collateral.

Capabilities are limited. As one person, you have only so much to give towards producing a product or providing a service. A business often requires the involvement of other people. It's not to say that sole proprietors can't operate large companies, but normally there are tax advantages to incorporating beyond a certain income level.

The company stops with you. Though you may employ other people, you as the sole proprietor are the decision maker. If you die, by law, your company no longer exists. It is possible, however, to will the business to someone else so that it can go on. Just make sure it is in writing and properly witnessed.

Partnerships

A partnership is the joint ownership of the business by two or more individuals or companies. Partnerships are not normally a good form of ownership for microbusinesses because these generally don't generate the kind of money needed to cover two or more management-level salaries. Making a good living for two partners plus workers is too much of a burden for the business unless that microbusiness earns net revenues greater than $300,000 a year.

EXAMPLE: *A microbusiness generates $150,000 a year (sometimes this is a lot for a microbusiness). The owner takes a salary of $50,000 and has overhead of $70,000, including wages for one or two employees and general operating expenses. There are taxes to consider, possible capital equipment needs. What amount would be left for other partners?*

There are a few advantages to partnerships. Like sole proprietorships, they are easy to form, with few government controls. Another advantage is that others are available to help make decisions and share in the work. Nevertheless, microbusiness owners, especially women, mistakenly tend to lean towards partnerships because of this support. But be aware that this decision may stem from lack of confidence in their ability to run the business or to make decisions alone. Partners in a microbusiness inevitably spend more time working on their relationship than on the business, causing the business to suffer, and sometimes causing its demise.

Some disadvantages of partnerships are:

Partnerships tend to break down, especially in a microbusiness situation where a small number of people try to control a small amount of money. Power struggles occur as people jostle for control because only one can realistically control the operation. The dynamics of the relationship ultimately bring down the operation.

The business is bound by the acts of all partners. If one person signs a contract obligating the business, then all partners are equally obligated under that arrangement. Even if a partner has only 25 percent ownership, she or he can obligate 100 percent of the owners. Plus, there is the unlimited liability issue. Litigation against the company can attach everything that each of the partners owns.

The key is to find support in other ways. Mentors, coaches or peer support groups all offering emotional support and information. Relying on a partnership to provide this level of support will only create problems.

Several alternatives offer support without the problems that accompany a partnership. One is to share profits with an employee rather than have a partner. Pay the person an agreed upon salary or other form of monetary compensation for work done. In addition, you can agree to share profits, once they begin. Remember the definition of profits: money that exists after paying all expenses, all salaries and all taxes. Be clear about how you will share the profits, and have it in writing.

Another alternative is to involve people as subcontractors. This way, you get the help and support you need running the business without the legal obligation of a partnership. You will pay less for their services and have fewer headaches overall.

If you are determined to form a partnership after having read this chapter, use the following guidelines:

- **Be clear as to the reasons you feel you need a partner, making sure it is not for emotional support.**

- **Make sure the partner balances a weakness of yours (more knowledge in a particular area, money you don't have, etc).**

- **Ask yourself if you could make it happen by yourself. If not, maybe you shouldn't be in business.**

- **Have an attorney create a partnership agreement that establishes roles and responsibilities of each partner and how the partnership will be dissolved, and that clearly details who owns what percentage of the business and why.**

On a professional as well as personal level, it is my opinion that partnerships DO NOT WORK for microbusinesses. They may last for a long time, but they do not work.

EXAMPLE: *In 1986, I met two partners who had just started publishing an annual directory of small businesses. I was immediately uncomfortable with the notion that they wanted to make $60,000 each and pay a staff of five. As expected, that didn't happen. For three years, they took turns receiving a salary because they could not even eke out $60,000 between the two of them, it was more like $25,000 total.*

Both partners made many sacrifices, but the relationship fell apart, each questioning the judgement of the other in any decision. They had reached an understanding early on in the business defining roles and responsibilities. But as difficulties mounted, trust left, frustration increased and the walls eventually tumbled down. The reality was that both made poor management decisions. Chief among them was that they failed to realize that the business could not support them both, particularly when they did not take on off-season protects.

Corporations

A corporation is a legal entity whose assets are kept separate from those of the company's owners and/or stockholders. A business can incorporate in the state in which it operates or in another state that may be less expensive. California, for example, is one of the most expensive states in which to incorporate, costing more than $1,000, depending on the fee of the attorney, if one is used.

One of the biggest advantages of incorporation is that any liabilities are limited to the corporation itself. Therefore, someone filing a lawsuit is only entitled to what is available from the corporation. Personal assets of the owners cannot be touched, except by the Internal Revenue Service for nonpayment of corporate or payroll taxes.

Another advantage to incorporation is that it is easier to secure capital because banks can attach the corporation's assets. If the corporation has many assets, banks look on this as favorable. (Small corporations with few assets will have a difficult time securing loans from banks.) The easy transfer of ownership is another plus for corporations. Stock certificates, which indicate the percentage of stock owned and the value of that stock, are easy to sell and exchange.

Disadvantages to incorporation are:

State controls. The state has the right to impose certain taxes and fees on businesses, including state income taxes, franchise taxes, unemployment taxes and workman's compensation taxes.

Federal controls. The federal government (any one of several different agencies) has the right to impose restrictions and guidelines concerning how you will operate a business. Additionally, fees and monitoring can have an impact on your ability to generate revenue and on what taxes must be paid for the corporation.

Expensive to form. In addition to the fees required to incorporate, there also is a double tax situation that arises in corporations. Corporation owners, who are also called stockholders, pay personal tax on their salaries, plus paying corporate taxes.

Within the scope of corporations, there is a designation called a "Subchapter S" corporation. This type of company is a regular corporation whose stockholders decide they want a special tax advantage in which the IRS allows the company to pay taxes as if it were a sole proprietor or partnership. The company can do this and still maintain the protection against liability that incorporation provides. It behooves a smaller corporation to do this only when income levels are relatively low. If income is very high, taxes for a S-corporation can actually be higher than for a C-corporation (the normal corporation).

Companies can switch from a C-corporation to an S-corporation within the first two years of operation, as long as they have not completed a second annual income tax filing. When income levels are such that the S-corporation is no longer advantageous (putting the owners in the highest individual tax bracket), companies can return to C-corporation status.

A drawback to the S-corporation model is that the government is extremely watchful as to the taxes you pay because you enjoy a significantly lower rate than as a C-corporation. Always be mindful of the appropriate time to revert to a regular C-corporation. Be sure that the higher income levels won't change (drop) drastically in the next few years to follow, such as from the loss of a major contract, or changing could be a mistake. Always seek guidance from a competent small business accountant. You can change status in each direction once, so be sure your action is the right one at the time.

Limited Liability Companies (LLCs) ━━━━━━━

The LLC is a unique and relatively new form of business organization that is treated as a partnership for income tax purposes and as a corporation for liability purposes. Check with your Secretary of State's office to see whether your state offers the limited liability company.

In an LLC, stockholders are called members, and they can manage the company without any personal liability. Anyone can buy membership, unlike corporations, which have restrictions as to who can own certain kinds of corporations. Another advantage to an LLC is that taxes are calculated, as in a partnership, based on the percentage of ownership. If you own 25 percent of the LLC, your share of taxes would be 25 percent. Moreover, you are taxed as if that 25 percent were personal income to you. The only significant disadvantage to an LLC is that they cost as much as regular C-corporations to form. Another restriction is that the life span of an LLC is determined from the onset and must be disclosed at the time of formation.

CHAPTER SIX

What Business Are You In?

While the title is bad grammar, it emphatically puts things into perspective immediately. Get clear about the answer! Hand in hand with deciding what form your business should take is clarifying exactly what your business is. Are you an inventor or a manufacturer, a temporary staffing agency or a computer training company? This kind of clarity helps you focus on performing the tasks necessary to make your business a success. Without it, you dilute your efforts and spread yourself too thin. When you have no clear direction, you actually jeopardize your chance of consistent income, stability, real growth and satisfaction. The first step in becoming clear is to understand your purpose.

Understanding Your Purpose

Whatever you attempt to do—in business or in personal life—always be conscious of your purpose for doing it. In starting a business, understanding your purpose can go a long way toward helping you identify exactly what you want to do and whom you want to target. Take the time to think through this short exercise.

EXERCISE. *Thinking of your business as a separate entity, answer these questions:*

Who are you? *What kind of business is it that you have? Is your company a marketing firm, a manufacturing company, a consulting service or a training agency?*

What do you do? *What services or products do you provide? Keep it succinct. Your response might be that you provide training services. Even more specific—and, therefore, better—is that you provide business training services.*

INTERSTATE

For whom do you do it? *This helps define your market. It's not good enough to say that you serve anyone. Be as specific as possible in identifying age bracket, gender, ethnicity, income bracket and any other pertinent details about who it is that uses the products or services you provide.*

What is the benefit? *Why are you doing what you do? Why do people buy your products or services? There has to be a benefit to what you do or no one would buy what you sell. For example, XYZ Company trains middle-income females to assist them in getting job promotions. Getting promotions is the benefit.*

Answering these four questions gives you a simple, quick phrase you can use when you are networking. It also helps you to sound articulate, professional and knowledgeable about your business. Thus, in response to the question "What do you do?" the owner of XYZ Company might respond: "XYZ is a career development training company that teaches middle-income females how to become more promotable in their careers."

By fine-tuning this four-question response, you will have a clear picture of your purpose, your market, your reason for existence. Consequently, so will others. This knowledge alone can bring you business. At the same time, not knowing how to answer these questions muddles your message and can turn away business. If you're having a hard time answering these questions, spend more time with them. Refocus, redefine and rework the questions—peel away the layers until you find the essence of what you do.

EXAMPLE: *A woman business owner was to be guest speaker at an event I helped to organized. The woman sent me her brochure to use in developing her biography for the program. I was amazed and dumfounded to discover how many services she offered, services that she identified as different businesses operated under one umbrella. Her business has to do with printing and embroidery of specialty items, and silk screening. She was billing herself as an advertising agency, a graphic art service, a silk screen printing shop and an embroidery company. The brochure was terribly confusing, but after examining it, I realized that she had one business. To operate a full-service promotional specialty business, she had to include all these other services.*

She was not clear about who she was, what she did or the benefit of it. She did not understand her purpose for being in business, thus she was unable to articulate this information in her marketing materials.

Feasibility

Feasibility is about survival. Don't take it lightly. It can determine whether you find financial assistance for raising capital, or whether you will fall flat on your face. Whether your business is feasible depends to a great extent on you, though there are always some circumstances over which you have no control. Remember that we live in a pared down economy. It's not the heyday of the early 1980s. Banks are not as free with their money, corporations are down-sizing, retail stores come and go in the blink of an eye. If a Jack in the Box or a McDonalds closes because a particular community can no longer afford to support it, what makes you think your business can survive in the same community?

Key Questions

To decide whether it is feasible for you to develop a certain product or service in a particular area or community, ask yourself the following questions. Doing so will give you a better sense of direction.

- **Is there a need or desire for your product or service?**
- **Who is the target market, and can it support your business?**
- **How many other such businesses serve the same market?**
- **Will the targeted group be willing to pay your price?**
- **What are the trends for this kind of business?**
- **What is the growth potential? Is it a fad?**
- **Where is the best location, based on the target market?**
- **How much start-up and operating capital is required, and can you provide it?**

These questions are all essential ones, not to be ignored or passed over. If you don't understand who your market is, you will never tap into it. Likewise, if you know your market but don't know what they're willing to pay for your product or service, you still may fail.

A personal experience brought this home to me, and I will never forget it. In 1991, I negotiated a deal with Northwestern University in Chicago to teach a microbusiness training program and to run it out of the university's adult education program (the University College). We priced the program at $695, which was equivalent to one course at the university level. We did lots of publicity for it, and I got 150 phone calls from small business owners or prospective business owners interested in taking the course. In most respects, it seemed an entirely feasible endeavor. But when registration time came, only seven people signed up for the course. I discovered that it wasn't that the remaining 143 didn't want it; they couldn't afford it. Although it was priced the same as university courses, they just didn't have the $695 to pay for the course. They were small business owners, struggling to pull their businesses together, and they knew it was exactly what they needed. But they couldn't pay that price. The class didn't run, and I lost thousands of dollars in advertising costs. I knew there was a need, but I failed to make sure the potential participants could pay the price I needed to charge.

This example underscores the importance of asking all of the key feasibility questions. Will the target group you've identified pay the price that you ask? If the answer is no, and a survey confirms that, you must reconsider whether it makes sense to start the business or offer the service or product. Having a good idea is not good enough. You need hard data to understand what is happening in your industry, the trends going on around you and the market you're seeking. A feasibility study provides this kind of crucial information. Even seasoned practitioners make careless mistakes. Learn from the mistakes of others; determine the feasibility first.

Feasibility Study

Doing a feasibility study can transform your business from a gamble to a risk. Without this background information, you may underestimate what it will take to make your business work. You may overestimate the appeal and affordability of your product or service and underestimate the amount of money you need to run the operation. This is like putting money in a slot machine. You spend the time, effort, money and energy to create a business, only to find out a few months down the road that it is not working.

EXAMPLE: *Horton Plaza is an award-winning shopping mall in downtown San Diego that has a stunning design. There are large anchor stores, such as Macy's and Nordstrom, and more than 100 smaller boutiques, restaurants and other specialty stores. For all its beauty, the plaza is laid out such that foot traffic does not go past all stores all of the time. Plus, many San Diegans do not shop at Horton Plaza because of the large number of homeless people in the downtown area. Thus, on any given day, you can walk through the plaza and see stores—primarily the smaller ones—closing and new ones opening. Wait six months and some of those new ones will be shutting down as well. Some stores come and go in as little as three or four months.*

The point is that many of these stores did not do feasibility studies. The businesses were simply a gamble. Had they done feasibility studies to assess their ability to survive in that plaza, many probably would not have opened.

A feasibility study can be as sophisticated as you have the money to make it, or as simple as a survey in person or by phone. Unless you go with the most sophisticated approach, the information these studies yield won't be scientific, but it will at least provide a clue as to whether your business has a chance to succeed.

A large part of your feasibility study will be a market survey. First, develop no more than six questions about what it is you are trying to accomplish. Decide who you will ask and whether it will be by phone or in person (on a busy street, in a mall, at a bus stop or in an office building lobby). Your survey will be most valuable if it specifically targets the individuals or companies to whom you intend to market. In addition to the questions, include demographic information on each form to determine age, gender, occupation, ethnicity, income or whatever is applicable to the situation. Always use a range in asking age and income questions.

Use a separate questionnaire for each respondent. For an informal survey, get at least 50 responses; 100 is better. The objective should be to have as many responses as possible.

Once you've obtained all your responses, sort the information according to demographic categories, and analyze the results. How many answered the questions? What percentage of those responding are interested in your product or service? What age range/income range is most interested?

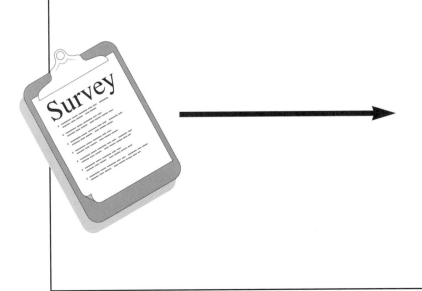

SAMPLE SURVEY QUESTIONNAIRE

Please assist us in creating a new business by completing the following questions.

Objective: To open a store to sell Western-style clothing for men, women and children.

1. Have you purchased any items of Western clothing in the past year?
    Yes_____ No_____

2. Is Western clothing (denim, fringe, studs, etc.) of any interest to you?
    Yes_____ No_____

3. Which items would be of interest to you: Women's ___ Men's___ Children's___
    shirts___ skirts___ pants___ jackets___

4. What would you be willing to pay for a shirt?
    $8-$14 (modest)___ $15-$25(low moderate)___
    $26-$50 (high moderate)___

5. How far would you be willing to travel to make this purchase?
    0-5 miles___ 6-10 miles___ 11-25 miles___

FOR OUR RECORDS:

Age: 18-25 ___   26-35____   6-50____   over 50____

Annual income: less than $20,000 ___ $21,000-$35,000___
$36,000- $50,000___   over $50,000_____

A feasibility study can also help you determine where to locate your business. If, for example, you want to sell a service generally purchased by large corporations, you may discover during your feasibility study that your town has no large corporate headquarters. To make your business succeed, you'll have to market to a nearby community that does.

To calculate whether you will have enough money to run the business in the manner suggested by your study it is necessary to research costs. Once you have collected information, you will need to prepare financial projections, complete with cash-flow analysis, before deciding whether you have the funds to start the business.

For pricing, include price ranges in any questionnaire or survey you develop (see sample). Setting a price/fee is based on several factors: what the market will bear, covering your expenses and giving you a profit. The questions on the survey will help you to understand what the market will bear. A cost analysis (discussed in Chapter Nine) must be completed before determining your costs.

What If It's Not Feasible?
What do you do when your feasibility study says "no go?" You've either got to be objective enough to recognize that your business idea isn't a good one, or you'll need to adjust your plan.

EXAMPLE: *One of my clients had a premature baby in 1995 and had tremendous difficulty finding baby clothing for her. She decided to open a mail-order company that would cater to the needs of premature babies. One of the first questions I asked her was: How feasible is such a business? How many premature babies are born annually in the county, state and country? Is the market large enough to justify setting up such a company? What is the probability of earning enough money to justify being in business? She had no answers but set out to find them, though she was unwilling to put the business on hold until then.*

After a long while, she obtained and interpreted the information. She discovered that even if 5 percent of her market actually purchased her goods (and 5 percent is a high rate), it translated to a very small revenue stream for the business. She decided to go ahead with her plan, in spite of what her statistics say and even if she makes only $10,000 to $15,000 a year. But, $10,000 to $15,000 a year does not a business make. It's not worth the enormous effort required to establish and maintain a business.

If she wanted to, this client could modify her business to make it more profitable. I encouraged her to think in terms of what else she could offer that would increase the market appeal of her products or of the company in general. She could offer clothing not just for low-birth-weight babies, but for extra large babies as well. They have special clothing needs, too, since they are not tall enough to fit into most clothing for older babies. Or, she could market to other cities across the country to increase her business potential. Another alternative is to incorporate other items into the product line that would appeal to a different segment of the infant wear market, such as infant sizes through one year. Eventually, she could generate up to $100,000 a year in revenue.

I strongly recommend against this client's approach. It provides very little return for a tremendous expenditure of energy. There is but one reason to be in business and that is to make a profit.

(And remember that profit is above and beyond all of your expenses, salary and overhead costs!) Feasibility should be the deciding factor in whether to move forward on your business idea or not at all.

Maintaining Your Focus

Once you've decided on your purpose and determined that your business idea is feasible, your job will be to maintain your focus and direction. It is sometimes tempting to veer in other directions, to take on projects other than the services or products you normally provide—especially if there is short-term revenue involved.

EXAMPLE: *sometimes inventors try to manufacture the items they invent to earn a larger percentage of the sales price. To do so, they would become responsible for a facility, equipment, workers, production schedules and countless other duties required to produce the invention. Minimum outlay to manufacture the item could be more than $200,000, which is beyond the capacity of many people. More importantly, attending to the details of manufacturing, marketing and deal-making may divert the energy and attention that the inventor needs to create—and creating is an inventor's lifeblood. A simple solution would be to contract out production and focus on the deal-making. The real question is: What business are you in, inventing or manufacturing?*

EXAMPLE: *A temporary staffing agency wanted to branch out into computer training. The owner reasoned that since the company already offered computer training to its temps, it could also offer it to clients. Again the necessary question: Is this company in the training business or the staffing business? Each business requires a different set of skills and focus. Trying to capture different targets dilutes the effort and diminishes the outcomes.*

Don't allow yourself to be swayed. Remember what business you are in. Focus strictly on what you do best, and learn to say no! If you own a business training company and somebody asks you to facilitate a retreat, refer that person to another company. Although it may be similar to what you do, it is not business training. And referrals often come back to you once companies recognize that you are sending business their way.

Going from one target market to another, taking on too many responsibilities and being pulled in many different directions, can scatter your efforts. That drains your energy and diminishes your effectiveness. You spend far more energy trying to keep up with different situations than you would with one consistent situation.

Plan your work and work your plan. Know what it is you have to offer. Know who buys your product or services, and focus on them. Make sure you are not trying to do too much. People are astute in recognizing someone who is not focused or clear—and they usually steer clear.

Naming Your Business

Your business name is the first thing people see about your company and, therefore, your first opportunity to market the business. Take time to think carefully about your name.

Too often, you see names such as "Joe Blow & Associates." After all, the large accounting and law firms do it. But a name like that is not only mildly egotistical, it simply doesn't let people know what you do. Whether yours is a marketing firm, a sales organization or a jeans manufacturer, the name should be representative of the business. Think of Guess Jeans, Skylight Photographic and Creative Kitchen Designs. The Women's Business Training Center gets countless phone calls because of its name; people looking in the phone book immediately get a sense of what it does.

In the ROSE Program (The ROad to Self-Employment) that I run, one participant had searched long and hard for a company name. She makes hand-crafted jewelry and originally decided to use her own name along with "fine jewelry" or "fine art jewelry", but the name was taken.

Weeks went by, and she returned with a new name: Ancient Elements. The name describes the technique she uses to create the jewelry. She wasn't sure it was exactly the right name, but she was tired of looking and hadn't found anything she liked any better. She decided she would register the name.

Not a week later, a new client came into the center who teaches belly dancing, an ancient form of body movement. The name of her company? Of course, it was Ancient Elements. Not tied to the name either, the belly dancer eventually changed her name, and the jewelry maker eventually changed hers. I encouraged both of them to add something to their names that would better describe the nature of the business, a tagline.

Think seriously about the name you want. People draw conclusions about your business based on its name. One client operates a boutique named Oceans International that sells clothing, gifts and accessories. She is always getting phone calls from people who think it's an import/export business. That won't happen if you provide enough information for people to draw the correct conclusion.

Taglines

Taglines are short, descriptive phrases that add information or meaning to your business name. They are useful in communicating effectively what you do or in conveying a certain image.

Think of all the major companies that use taglines with their names.

- **Coca-Cola—"It's the real thing."**

- **Burger King—"Have it your way."**

- **Maxwell House Coffee—"Good to the last drop."**

- **American Express—"Don't leave home without it."**

- **U.S. Marines—"The few, the proud, the brave."**

- **Timex (watch)—"It takes a licking and keeps on ticking."**

Some less common examples include:

- KMN Growth Consultants—"Coaching businesses to greater profits."

- Women's Business Training Center—"Turning ideas into reality."

- The Internet Connection—"Custom on-site, on-line training services."

- A Bride's Guide—"The one-stop shop for brides."

- Mountain Dome Studio—"Sendable/Frameable Art."

Taglines are simple phrases that help to clarify what a company does or how it does it. They are effective tools in helping consumers remember who you are or what you do. They often help to distinguish you from your competition. Taglines enhance your image by presenting the illusion that you are a large, prosperous company that can afford to pay creative people to develop your materials.

Logos

A logo should tie together the company name and tagline to create a professional image with which others can readily identify. A clever logo will go a long way toward getting you in the door and having your product or service accepted. It is your visual aid in marketing. It's often worth hiring a professional to design one for you.

Logos are not just about cute little pictures or stylish lettering; they're about sending messages, creating an image. Far too many logos have nothing at all to do with the person's business. Work on the vision first, on the image or impression you want the logo, name and tagline to create. Do you want to look crisp and professional or soft and homey? Will your total look convey that quality matters or that aesthetic beauty is important? Or, does your logo need to be pragmatic and utilitarian? Whatever you come up with, make sure that it depicts what your business does. It doesn't have to be fancy or expensive, but it does need to deliver the right message.

If you don't have much money to spend on the logo, consider hiring a graphic art or drawing student at a local college or university. They're usually willing to work for a small amount of money to build their portfolio. Ask to see samples of their work, and make sure they have access to and experience with the equipment necessary to do the job. If you don't know any students, post a notice on a campus bulletin board or call the art department for referrals.

A good logo will pay for itself many times over, so don't hedge on the cost just to save a few dollars. If you have the funds available, invest in a good image for your business. If you're not satisfied with the finished product, don't accept it. By the same token, be as clear with the artist as you possibly can about what you want.

Naming and framing your business is your first opportunity to make an impression. Names, logos and taglines become your advance marketing team, your front line. Don't miss or misuse this opportunity! Take the time to develop something you can live with for a long time to come. A professional logo should last for 20 years or more.

Developing a Business Structure

You might be the only person running your business when it starts, but for your business to grow, you will need to involve other people. When you do, you need to have a structure in place so that you can begin to allocate tasks and responsibilities to them, be they full-time employees, subcontractors or part-time workers.

Structuring your business properly helps you to be in control of it. You will understand what tasks must be done to move the business forward and who will be responsible for which tasks. Even if you're the only one working at the beginning, it's helpful to have clear delineations for the responsibilities of operating that business. For example, what are the tasks involved with marketing the business? With administration? Know the different roles and responsibilities of running a business, and keep them separate in your mind.

It's important to get all this down in writing. Doing so gives you a visual road map; you see exactly where you're going and what

you have to do to get there. Develop an organizational chart like the one below, projecting it out three years. You might end up with two or three charts. Or, if you use just one, as pictured, indicate those positions which will not start for another year or two.

Once you know the different tasks, break them down into individual responsibilities. For record keeping tasks, you may assign some

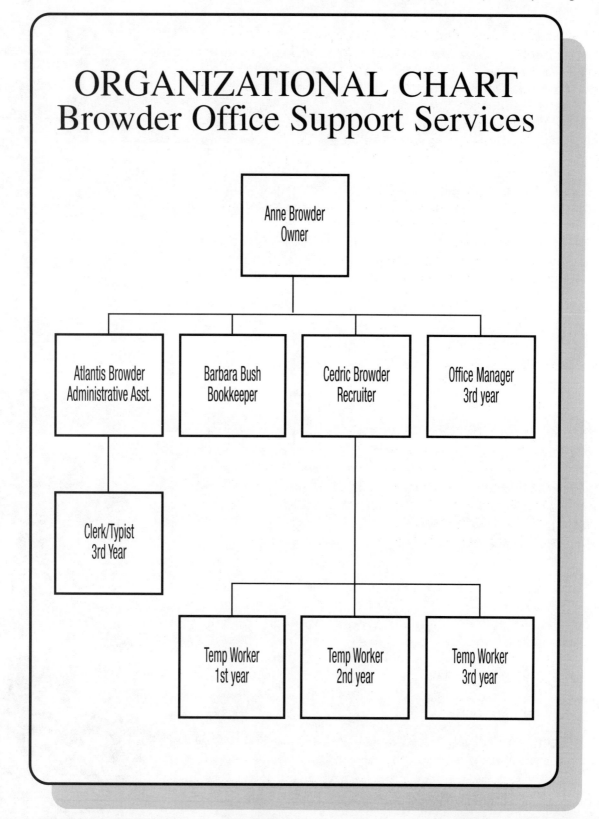

ORGANIZATIONAL CHART
Browder Office Support Services

Anne Browder
Owner

Atlantis Browder
Administrative Asst.

Barbara Bush
Bookkeeper

Cedric Browder
Recruiter

Office Manager
3rd year

Clerk/Typist
3rd Year

Temp Worker
1st year

Temp Worker
2nd year

Temp Worker
3rd year

of the individual responsibilities to an accountant or bookkeeper. Or you may hire sales representatives to handle marketing tasks. Working through the organizational chart helps you think in terms of who will do what. As its name implies, the organizational chart helps you be more organized, which helps you to plan your work.

Some tasks you will prefer over others. This is natural, but don't allow yourself to skip tasks just because you don't enjoy doing them or don't understand how to do them. You owe it to yourself to give your business every opportunity to succeed. When you give less than 100 percent, you hurt no one but yourself! Find someone to teach you what you don't know. For those tasks you'd rather not do, hire someone. Or, if money is an issue, try bartering—trade some of your products or services for work. Get creative in your approach to getting the job done.

If you're stuck for ideas or looking for alternatives, seek help. One avenue is a small business assistance center. There may be several in your community. Services are free and usually available on a regular basis, if needed. Such centers are often called Small Business Development Centers or SBDCs. The federal Small Business Administration (SBA) also administers the Service Corps of Retired Executives, or SCORE, a volunteer team of consultants, usually men, who are former business executives. SCORE exists in every city where the SBA has an office. Most of these volunteers provide information geared to a particular area of business, such as marketing, finance or accounting. They are usually very helpful when you have specific needs and questions.

While SCORE and SBDC are a good place to start, they aren't geared for in-depth assistance. For overall assistance, professional business consultants, coaches, accountants and technicians will provide more solid information. Find one who can guide and assist you or hook up with a mentor. However you choose to gain assistance, seek the information you need to develop a sound business structure.

CHAPTER SEVEN

Working Smart

This chapter offers you six ways to get ahead and stay ahead of your business. These bits of information are vital links to success. Absorb each section, complete each exercise, and learn the subtle differences that will put you miles in front of your competition and truly allow you to work <u>smart</u> in running your business.

Separating Yourself From Your Business

You need separation from your business to objectively analyze what it needs, what needs changing, what decisions must be made. Separating is not an easy thing to do, particularly when you are the only person operating the business. But when you are unable to separate yourself, you jeopardize your chances of success.

I often advise clients to think of their business as a child. When your business is newly born, you devote all of your attention to nurturing, nourishing and protecting it. As your "baby" grows, it starts to take on a life of its own. It begins to want its own independence and to operate without you being around so much.

As in a child's life, other people start to play important roles in your business's life. Maybe not at first, but certainly after a year or two, you should begin to allow others to understand the workings of the business. You begin to focus your energies on something else, business-related or not. You might want to take on personal goals, such as traveling, retirement, writing a book or having a baby. Or you might need time away from the daily demands of running a business to investigate expanding your operations. It doesn't mean that you give the business up or lose control of it, just that you gain some healthy distance and objectivity.

Preparing your business for other people's involvement means making sure they know how to run the business properly, generating enough revenue and caring well for clients or customers. If you don't take the time to do this, then prepare to fail. If you don't step back from the business, how do you ever expect to lie on the beach at Waikiki without the business falling apart? You've spent the money, energy and commitment thus far on your business. Why jeopardize your success by ignoring this important separation process? For the sake of the business, for its continuation, and for your peace of mind, you must begin to think of the business as an entity separate from you.

Business Succession

Most small business owners never give much thought to whether a business will continue after their death. Indeed, if you are a sole proprietor, the business is no longer a legal entity after you die. The same process by which you separate from your business also can help you to prepare the business to continue after you are gone.

> ...be honest with yourself and realize that you can't do it all.

Take the time to train someone. Perhaps it is the person you have allowed to become most involved in the business. Or perhaps it is a family member. It's best to let that person know that you are grooming him or her to take over the business. Whomever you choose to prepare, be sure to leave written instructions. Get legal assistance to ensure that the instructions become a legal document. Keep a copy with your will or personal papers.

If you don't take the time to consider the continuation of your business, it is likely to fall into the hands of people who don't care, or who will misuse or destroy what you have worked so very hard to achieve. If you don't care, they won't either—guaranteed!

Employees vs. Subcontractors

If you don't know your strengths and weaknesses before you begin your business, you soon will. Business ownership has a way of highlighting one's limitations. But don't view this as a negative. Simply be honest with yourself and realize that you can't do it all. Your very next step is to get help.

Help doesn't have to come in the form of employees. Subcontracting is an inexpensive and convenient way of getting things done without having a payroll. Subcontractors are people who perform tasks at a site other than your facility or who incur the expense of doing the work. You pay subcontractors based on an agreement, whether hourly or flat fee, and you are not obligated to deduct taxes or report them as employees. However, if you pay a subcontractor more than $600 in a year, you must file tax form number 1099 with the Internal Revenue Service.

Subcontractors work only when you need them—no long-term commitments. Working with subcontractors frees up your time to devote to other projects—whether that's the day-to-day business operation, sales, errands or working with clients. Temporary workers also are considered subcontractors. One last note about subcontractors: The IRS has a publication to help you determine the difference between subcontractors and employees. Make sure to follow all legal guidelines regarding subcontractors versus employees.

An alternative to subcontracting is to hire part-time workers to take care of the "busywork" that your company generates. For example, you might hire someone two days a week to file papers, make copies, assemble materials for a mailing, type in a database, etc. Before you dismiss this idea as unaffordable, do the following exercise.

EXERCISE: *Make a list of all the busywork that needs doing in your company (or prospective company). Think of things that don't absolutely need your involvement, tasks that don't generate revenue. Estimate how many hours a week the work will take and multiply that by the hourly rate that you're willing to pay someone else to do the work. Now assess the dollar value of your own time. That would be the hourly rate that you charge clients or your weekly salary divided by the number of hours a week that you work. Multiply your hourly rate by your estimate of hours per week to complete the busywork. Compare your total to the total for an outside person, and ask yourself this question: Can I afford not to hire a part-time person to take care of these tasks?*

Under most circumstances, you'll find that you save money and energy by hiring a part-time person. Hiring someone to do the non-revenue-generating tasks allows you to focus on bringing in revenue. It's a good way to work <u>smart</u>.

Another <u>smart</u> concept is to use messenger or delivery services whenever possible. Tally up all the time you spend in an average week delivering and picking up things. Think of the money you could earn during that time doing revenue-generating work. Compare this to the cost of a messenger service. Much like the part-time worker, you would probably end up earning money by hiring a messenger service.

SWOT Exercise (Strengths, Weaknesses, Opportunities, Threats)

This is an exercise recommended to clients to help them assess strengths and weaknesses (internal factors they have some control over), and opportunities and threats (external factors over which they have less control).

EXERCISE: *Take a piece of paper and fold it once vertically so that you end up with four columns, counting the front and the back. At the top of each of the four columns, list a SWOT category. Do this twice, for you personally and for the business. Working with one column at a time, think about that particular element. For example, in one column, list your strengths, using only words and phrases, not sentences.*

Don't do this exercise in one sitting. Focus on one aspect at a time over the course of a week or two. As you think about different traits, write them in the appropriate columns.

This exercise will help you explore areas you may not have considered before. For example, your weakness might be not knowing how to market your company. However, your strength might be meeting people and putting them at ease. This could help you understand that you have the confidence but not the knowledge to market your product. Get some help. There are plenty of marketing consultants out there and extensive resource materials. If you feel weak in record keeping or accounting, there are plenty of bookkeepers, accountants or others who can help you with the financial aspects of the business.

In the areas of opportunities and threats, be introspective. For example, under opportunities, think of where your opportunities lie: your knowledge, contacts, experience, even the business's location. Under threats, list situations that could throw a wrench into the works, for example, the economy or your health.

By being aware of these four areas, you will be prepared to deal with them when they arise. Do not be a sleeper! Knowing where the opportunities are will help you reach out and grab them; being aware of possible threats will help you avoid or deal with them. By working smart, you prepare yourself. You can turn those threats into challenges that do not deter you from moving your business forward.

STOP

STOP
LOOK
LISTEN

Keeping Track of Your Market ▬▬▬▬

Once you have determined your target market, you must continue to evaluate that market. Things change, including who might buy from you.

EXAMPLE: *Your research tells you that men between the ages of 18 and 30 with an income of $30,000+ are your target market and you design you strategies accordingly. You leave flyers at a fitness center, make presentations at recreational facilities and go online to reach them via the Internet.*

If you keep track of who is actually buying your product, extracting and analyzing the data properly, you may come to discover that your target market is slightly off or that it has changed. It may be men 25 to 40 years old earning $40,000+. If you continue to target the younger group, you may be putting the wrong kind of material out in the wrong place through the wrong sources. You may continue to do business, but you won't be reaching as many customers as possible and thereby will not maximize your profits.

EXAMPLE: *A car wash was using newspaper advertising, handing out flyers in the mall and putting flyers on parked cars. Business was good but not increasing proportionally to the amount spent on marketing. The owner conducted an informal survey over several weeks and asked customers what brought them into the car wash. The survey revealed that the car wash sign was the most effective advertising tool—and not the flyers or the more expensive newspaper ads. The owner lighted his sign, made it larger and doubled his profits within a few months.*

Know your market. That is a key element necessary for your success. Keep your ear to the ground and study the information you collect from clients and customers, to find out how you can market more effectively.

Pricing Services and Products ▬▬▬▬

It is vital to understand all of the costs involved in delivering your service/product and operating your business before setting your price. By performing a cost analysis and understanding your expenses, you are more aware of what it takes to succeed and, consequently, more in control of your business.

When done for pricing purposes, a cost analysis should include not just the expenses you normally pay each month, but all costs you will incur to operate a profitable business. For example, even if you can't afford to pay health insurance, calculate it into the analysis since you will never be able to afford it if it is not built into the price you charge. Likewise, you must build in a profit if you expect to ever make one.

First, list all your expenses, either on a weekly, monthly or annual basis. If, for example, your cost analysis is to be on a monthly basis, you would total your monthly expenses—salary, product manufacturing costs, wages, office costs, marketing, etc. Prorate any annual or long term expense, e.g. computers, office furniture, equipment, taxes, depreciation, fringe benefits, etc.

EXAMPLE: *If you paid $3,000 for a computer and printer, you may only depreciate it for three years since the technology changes so rapidly. Divide the total paid into thirty-six months and the monthly expense is $83.33 This amount would be used even if you paid in one payment. Other equipment can be depreciated over six years. The accounting rule of thumb is: If it costs more than $200, it is considered equipment, otherwise it is classified as supplies or tools. Be sure to list all expenses, current or anticipated, to cover expenses and make a profit.*

To the total of your monthly costs, add a percentage for contingency costs, a cushion in case things go wrong (usually $100 to $500). Be aware of the industry standard for profit margin and incorporate that profit into your cost analysis. Remember, you're in business to make a profit!

To cover unexpected expenses, you need to build in a contingency, a cushion in case things go wrong. Also, be aware of the industry standard for profit margin and incorporate that profit into your cost analysis. Next, break down your expenses, either on a weekly, monthly or annual basis.

Once you have a total, divide the number of products that you produce in a month or total average billing hours to give you an average selling price/fee. This price, however, is based on you selling that amount of product every month, or billing a particular number of hours if you are a service business. If, for example, you are not selling all of that product or billing all the needed hours, then all of your expenses would not be met. Here is where the contingency fund comes into play. This explains why you may not make a profit every month or why you might not be able to take all of your salary at times.

When you are not generating the total of the cost analysis, you will have to cut expenses. By performing the cost analysis and understanding your expenses, you are in control of your business, and you will be able to see what needs to be done. If the price/fee you determine through the cost analysis is out of line with the market rates, you must find ways to cut back on your expenses in order to be competitive. Don't eliminate your salary, find ways to trim back on other expenses so that you can still have a salary, if not literally then at some point in the future.

In a retail operation, it is imperative to use a formula for calculating a price, as completing cost analysis for each item sold is nonproductive. However, an overall cost analysis to determine how much is needed from the business to cover necessary expenses is required. Formulas for pricing individual items make life easier—but make sure your formula will include all your expenses. Typical markups (formulas) for retail are double (keystone), 2.2 or 2.5 (multiply your cost of the item by 2.2 or 2.5).

Never, ever, pull a number out of the air and say this is the price/fee you are going to charge. Your expenses will be different from everyone else's and you must factor all your expenses into the price of your product. Take the time to detail how you will make pricing adjustments in the future.

Compare your price to the competition only after you have conducted the cost analysis. If your price is higher than that of the competition, don't panic. This is usually because you cannot buy in large quantity and pay a higher price for services you receive. Be fair about your pricing, but always make sure you have an opportunity to make a profit!

PROCEED WITH CAUTION

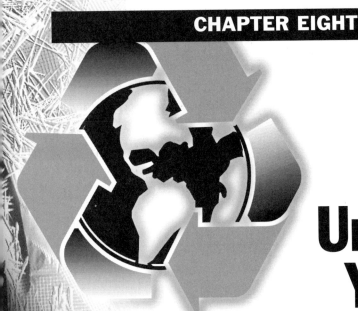

CHAPTER EIGHT

Understanding Your Industry

To operate your business effectively, you must first understand your industry—the success factors, the trends, the skills needed for success and the practicality of the particular industry. You must also know your industry's critical market segments.

Because there are so many sub categories within a given industry, you'll need to conduct thorough research to understand where you fit as a microbusiness owner. If you want to be a player, you need to know your industry. Do your research before starting your business.

Six important concepts to know about an industry are outlined in this chapter. Know them well so that you make wise business decisions. Keep current on trends within your industry. Read trade publications and other current literature; get involved in the associations and organizations key to your industry. You'll stay on top of—not behind—your industry's trends.

Six important concepts to know about your industry:

The Size and Nature of Your Industry

First, learn the actual size, as well as the potential size, of your industry. You will understand where you fit in when you know the number of businesses and the revenue generated in your industry. Find out as much as you can about key players and about your competition. Good sources of information are the U.S. Census Bureau (part of the Department of Commerce), trade associations, periodicals and Department of Labor information. Other sources: Robert Morris & Associates and Dun & Bradstreet both publish information you can find in the library reference section or on the Internet.

In researching, be cognizant of sales figures for the particular product line or service you plan to offer. Look for growth of major players, and study the geographic factors. For example, in Chicago, a business consultant could easily charge $125 an hour for working with small business owners. Yet in San Diego, the market would only bear $75 per hour for the same client base. Learn the differences that exist geographically for what you are trying to accomplish.

Who makes up your market segment, and what is the disposable income of your potential customers? Look for niches you can fill. But remember: Your fresh idea is great only if you can make it happen.

...competition is healthy...

Recognize names that are key to your industry and what kind of power exists that you can play off of or use to your advantage. Find out if there are financial resources available by virtue of your membership in that industry. Look at product loyalty. Perhaps people will buy your product because it has an established track record within the industry or is similar to another well-established product. Small franchise operations or distributorships might be an option; for example, Decorating Den, Merle Norman Cosmetics or Creative Memories.

Competition

It is important to remember that competition is healthy and that you can learn valuable lessons from your competitors.

There are two kinds competition: direct and indirect. A direct competitor is someone selling the same product or service, or a very similar one, to the same market as you. A competitor selling the same product or service in a completely different market—for example, in another town to a different clientele—represents indirect competition. Know your competition and whether there is potential for new competition, both direct and indirect.

EXAMPLE: *An operator of a small snack shop in one part of town might sell tacos while a shop similar in size and clientele sells barbecue. Both are in the restaurant industry; fast food or take-out is the subindustry. They are indirect competitors, but they could learn from each other since they cater to a target market that probably has very similar demographics. How do they market? How much do they pay workers? What hours are they open? Average sale? Suppliers? These are a few of the questions that would benefit each, even though they service different markets.*

Examine your indirect competitors to find out how they deliver the product or service. Examine your direct competitors to find out what kind of wages they pay to make sure that your standards of operation and quality assurance are not lower than theirs.

Some questions you need to answer about direct competition:

- **What is the competition like?**

- **What is the potential for new competition entering the marketplace?**

- **Do new competitors enter the arena consistently and at what rate?**

Study your competition. This can be challenging since many microbusinesses cannot afford to advertise and you may not know they exist. One way to investigate your competition is to pose as a customer, or have someone else pose as a potential client, to discover the following:

- **The marketing materials your competition uses,**

- **The price range within which they operate,**

- **The kind of customer service they provide,**

- **The quality of the product or service they provide and if they guarantee their work,**

- **The customer base.**

If you can, find out whether their customers are satisfied with the merchandise or services provided. Don't think for a moment that your price needs to match or be lower than your competitor's. It's important to understand your costs before setting prices. Microbusinesses have a difficult time matching price while still making a profit. Provide "value-added" services even if a product is sold; this will justify any difference between your price and theirs.

Getting inside information on what the competition is planning to do can help you make changes or adjustments to keep up with the competition. Competition will keep you on your toes as much as it does your competitor. And it's healthy for the country; it keeps prices competitive, quality at a certain level and ensures that consumers get their money's worth.

Industry Growth Prospects

What is the potential of your industry—is it growing or stagnant? The manufacture of typewriters, for example, is not a booming business. Even someone who invented a fantastic new kind of typewriter might want to think twice about investing time, money, energy and effort in manufacturing it—and to think whether that same energy could be focused on computers. If you are dealing with typewriters, electronic memory typewriters are certainly more in demand than manual typewriters or even electric typewriters. This concept is known as segmented sales.

What are the segments of the industry in your niche, and what are the growth patterns within that segment? What about demographic data? Who buys your product, and is the demographic data and profile of the potential customer in a strong growth segment for the industry? Does it have an historical presence? These are all factors to be weighed. You may find after some research that you belong in a different segment of your industry, one with a positive growth pattern. It is certainly better to discover this sooner than later.

...be aware of the up-and-down trends of costs in your industry.

Structure of Your Industry: Suppliers, Cost, Distribution

Industry structure is the foundation and framework of the industry; the various businesses that depend on one another to create demand for products and services. For garments to be made, there must first be fabrics, thread, designs, machinery and equipment.

Suppliers are a cornerstone of industry structure. Find out as much as you can about your industry's suppliers, for their prices and practices affect your product and prices. Sometimes suppliers are able to monopolize their corner of the market in a particular geographic area, despite government regulations. For example, if you wanted to own billboards and sell advertising for billboards and bus benches, in some cities there is one company that dominates the industry.

As for cost, be aware of the up-and-down trends of costs in your industry. For example, the rising cost of paper has severely affected the publishing and printing industries. Ask yourself what raw materials are necessary for your business, and investigate the current situation for processing, assembling, and distributing your product. Look at current production levels in your industry, and determine whether they are increasing or decreasing.

You also need to see if developing countries are producing similar products. This often lowers the cost of production, but doesn't necessarily lower the price the consumer pays. To compete with such strategies, you must mass produce in tremendous quantities, something most microbusinesses cannot do. Can you compete with the same or similar products produced abroad at a fraction of the cost?

Look at the distribution channels within your industry. What are the current channels, and what alternative channels are likely to emerge in the future? Are there jobbers or brokers involved? A jobber is a middle person who usually sells products wholesale to those who will resell it. Jobbers usually allow you to purchase a smaller quantity than you can order directly from the manufacturer. Often a broker will do the same thing. The broker, however, does not normally have merchandise or services on hand, but will find something you need and usually has a wide base of suppliers.

Both jobbers and brokers add to your overall cost of production. Substantial additions to your cost will increase your selling price and reduce your profit margin.

Trends and Development

Understanding industry trends will put you ahead of the game. Know what is important: What needs are not being met, what new strategies are competitors using, and what new trends exist for distribution? Check to see if sales are tapering off because the industry is starting to die out.

The defense industry is a good example. Many microbusinesses subcontract with companies serving the defense industry. The defense industry has been downsizing for several years now. Suppliers and subcontractors are now having to find other uses and other target markets for their equipment and services. By realizing that the defense industry was taking a nose dive, many companies were able to regroup quickly without losing money. By the time their defense industry contracts had been fulfilled, they had mapped out new strategies to revamp their products/services and go after a different target market.

Certain segments of the retail market provide another example of a diminishing market. If you are a small retailer, you need to be especially aware of trends in your industry. You may even find ways to capitalize on large retail operations going out of business.

The Impact of Technology

Almost every industry is being impacted by rapidly changing technology and by the computer. Technology is making the business of doing business much easier. You can pay bills and do other banking functions via the computer. And information that used to involve a trip to the library or time-consuming research can now be readily accessed via the Internet on your home computer or at the library.

Technology is also impacting distribution channels. Cable companies are beginning to provide phone service, while phone companies are providing computer support services and more. It's important to know the technological trends in your industry and to determine whether these trends could help or harm you. Being able to predict technological advances will put you ahead of your competition.

In summary, understanding these six key features of your industry will benefit you before you decide what business to enter, and it will benefit you while you are in business. Staying aware of trends and shifts in your industry will keep you ahead of your competition.

CHAPTER NINE

Operational/ Organizational Systems

If you want your small business to grow and flourish, you must have operational systems. They will form the basis of your infrastructure and create a foundation on which to build your business. Systems allow you to plan for the future and not have to shift gears every time you meet a new problem. Instead, you will be able to focus on how to be profitable.

Many small business owners don't see the need for systems and believe that operating "by the seat of their pants" will work for a one-or two-person operation. This belief can lead to trouble down the road when the business begins to grow. With systems in place, a growing business can achieve peak productivity and success.

One important reason for systems is that as your business grows, you will need to bring in outside people. When things are written down, they don't need to be explained over and over, wasting your time and energy. Developing systems from the very beginning will increase your capacity to handle multiple tasks and be effective in the process. Then you will be well accustomed to using them as your business grows and the need for systems increases.

The following systems will allow you to work <u>smart</u>, while conserving your energy and maximizing productivity. Think of the future when you design your systems and know that you will be developing and redesigning these systems as your business changes.

Informational Systems

Information is power. Informational systems allow you to make decisions to grow a successful business. It can be as simple as 3 x 5 cards on clients or as detailed as a computer database will allow. Informational systems include forms, logs, reports, questionnaires, evaluation forms or anything else that helps you be more efficient. One important tip: Don't wait until later. The best time to record any data you collect—on clients, employees, vendors, contractors or anyone you see on a regular basis—is now. When you need that vital piece of information, it will be there waiting for you.

CUSTOMERS/CLIENTS. Maintain a file on every client or customer. If you run a retail operation, a simple 3 x 5 card on each of your regular customers will allow you to record pertinent information. You can use that information to contact them when there is a sale or when a particular item of merchandise arrives in the store. Having that kind of information filed and logically organized (alphabetical, zip code, etc) can increase profit by a large percentage—if the system is properly used.

If you provide a service, every client should have a file. Develop a standard form and name it anything you like (e.g., registration form or a client information sheet). List pertinent information about each client.

VENDORS. Every vendor or supplier you do business with should have a file. This file could include a copy of all invoices, information about what services or products were purchased from the vendor, and payment arrangements or other agreements. These records are vital for your business. And, if you are not available, your employees can refer to these records when dealing with vendors.

EMPLOYEES. Having records on employees is mandatory by law. You must keep pertinent files with each employee's social security number, U.S. citizenship information, picture identification, tax forms, any warnings or disciplinary action taken and personnel records in general. Attendance records should also be a part of an employee's file, along with evaluations they have received. If you use subcontractors instead of, or in addition to, employees, you should have a file on each of them, listing social security number, address and phone number.

EVALUATION FORMS. Evaluation forms can be used in a number of ways. They allow you to find out how your customers or clients feel about the products/service you provide. This is valuable feedback to help you build a better business. Internal evaluations help assess the performance of an employee or help you determine whether a particular system is effective.

General Record Keeping Systems

General record keeping systems help you make effective business decisions. In addition, record keeping is necessary for government audits and documentation for tax records. Keep current files with documentation of your business licenses, business name registration and other important papers.

CORRESPONDENCE AND AGREEMENTS FILES. Keeping a copy of all correspondence and signed documents can save you a lot of heartache and expense. Having copies of all of your correspondence will be to your advantage in the event of a dispute or discrepancy. I had a client in my office recently with a discrepancy concerning her lease. She believed she could use her deposit as the last month's rent; the property manager told her the lease contained a clause forbidding it. My client believed herself to be an organized person; however, she either did not have or could not find a copy of the lease. This error cost the client $1,000—an amount most microbusiness owners cannot afford to lose. Record keeping must be systematic to be effective.

RESEARCH FILES. Maintain records of all research you do. Market research information is beneficial, not just at the time that you collect it, but for years to come. Always maintain files on associates and on networking materials, as well as on information about your industry and any related information that helps you. Get in the habit of clipping articles or downloading them from the Internet about your industry or about business development. Maintain a file for such information and build a resource folder or binder for such materials. Press releases and articles written about your company should also be included in a file.

Operational Systems

Operational systems allow you to set policies and procedures with which to run your business in an effective and efficient manner.

ACCOUNTING SYSTEMS. Every business needs an adequate system of recording income and expense, assets and liabilities. Without it, chaos results. Your time and energy is far too valuable to spend it chasing numbers, worrying about bank balances, searching for receipts—and not running your business. An accountant can assist you in setting up your record keeping system and explaining how to maintain it. Other accounting systems include check files, ledgers and journals. Whatever you do, don't throw these records into a shoebox and forget about them until tax time.

BUDGETS. You can have budgets for many different things, such as marketing or purchasing. If you are a retail business, purchasing would be a critical budget for you to maintain. If you have a large operation, you might have budgets broken down by department. Maintaining files on all of these budgets will help you develop a strong system. Combined, they form an overall budget—a snapshot of the future—to help you know where you're going.

INVENTORY SYSTEMS. These systems allow you to know, at any given time, the status of your inventory. They include purchases made, delivery times, stock or inventory on hand, inventory on order, etc. If you are in retail or are a manufacturer with a number of component parts to track, an inventory system is an absolute must.

FINANCIAL REPORTS. These are usually done on a monthly basis. If you are a microbusiness, semi-annual or annual financial reports will probably suffice. Either way, it's necessary to know what is happening with your finances at all times, so monthly financial reports can be beneficial. These reports are for your sake, not to satisfy some external requirement. Creating a picture of your financial situation on a regular basis allows you to make better business decisions.

TAX RECORDS. Any tax item needs to have documentation. Establish a separate file to maintain such records.

PETTY CASH, ACCOUNTS PAYABLE, ACCOUNTS RECEIVABLE. Maintain files of invoices and statements, along with notations of when they were paid. You can never be in control if you are not aware of who owes you what, whom you owe and how much cash is available at any given time. Follow the guidance of an accountant in setting up this system.

Price/Fee-Setting Systems

Establishing a price/fee system is a must. It should all start with a cost analysis—understanding what your expenses are and making sure you can pay them. Be sure to incorporate a salary for yourself as well as your staff (including part-time and contract workers). *Understand that you will never make a profit if your cost analysis is not built into the pricing structure.*

By understanding what your expenses are and doing a cost analysis to break them down, you can objectively review them. You'll begin to realize why you need to set prices at a certain level. If you structure your price using a formula, I strongly recommend that you make sure that the prices you set cover your expenses.

I led a workshop recently and one participant told the story of how, when he left the military after the Vietnam War, he saw a vacant gas station in his neighborhood and decided to open it.

This man first investigated the area and discovered that there were several other gas stations, whose owners all charged the same price for gas. He figured it would be really smart to charge three cents less per gallon. He got the business up and running. The first month, as he reviewed his financial records, he found that he did not have enough money to cover all of his expenses.

He could not figure it out because he was pumping gas like crazy and had consistent customers. After the second month, he was further in the hole and by the third month, he was forced to close the business. Why? He had never bothered to do a cost analysis to understand whether charging three cents less per gallon would allow him to meet his expenses. Doing a cost analysis before you start to use any kind of formula will save you a lot—perhaps even your business.

As part of your price-setting system you should also list guidelines for increasing or decreasing your prices. Raising prices is something that should be done only after much deliberation. A price increase is a red flag to the consumer, many of whom will go an extra mile to save 10 cents, even if that extra mile costs them a quarter to travel. So it is important to have established guidelines dictating when to raise a price and how not to alienate customers or clients.

Purchasing Systems

Purchasing systems apply especially to retail operations. Your purchasing plan is a result of calculating an annual budget and deciding what you expect to sell and how much money you have to buy needed goods and/or services.

Your budget should clearly show how much is available for the whole year—but you must understand enough about your market to know when the purchasing is best. There is a concept in retail called "open to buy." This means the portion of your budget within a time frame that has not yet been utilized and is available for purchases.

Purchase orders and receiving records are also parts of a purchasing system. Purchase orders allow you to keep track of orders placed by individuals in your business. Microbusinesses often don't have the need for them, but if more than two or three people are ordering merchandise from various sources, you may want to use these forms. Receiving records can take on different forms–logs, packing list files, computer databases, etc. If you do receive goods on a regular basis, establish a system for maintaining records.

Security Systems

Often, microbusiness owners are so busy trying to tend the business that they never realize they might have something worth protecting. That's where security systems come in.

Security systems encompass a number of different practices, including keeping certain files locked, either at home or in a commercial facility. But one of the most important security functions is to protect information critical to your business—anything of a proprietary nature—with a trademark, service mark, copyright or patent.

A trademark protects logos, taglines, symbols or a word—all individual items, written or graphic, describing the name of a product. A service mark is equivalent to the trademark, but is for a service rather than a product. A copyright protects a body of work (written, music or art objects), while a patent protects an invention with all the specifications, formulas or technology required to produce it. Take the necessary steps to protect your business. Information on trademarks, service marks or copyrights is available in the appendix of this book, at the public library and on the Internet.

Policies and Procedures

Policies and procedures are processes and guidelines for operating a business effectively. Like your entire organizational/operational system, these policies are your foundation, so that the "rules" of your business are written down clearly and in place, offering guidelines for every situation that occurs.

Three areas for which I recommend policies and procedures.are:

EMPLOYEES AND CONTRACTORS.

The kinds of policies or decisions you might need to develop in this area include the following:

Job descriptions. These are necessary for every task performed in your business. You, as the business owner, may perform four or five different tasks. You should clearly describe and distinguish each of these functions so that, as your business grows, you can hire people to take on these responsibilities.

Hiring policies. Spell out just what kind of company guidelines you will follow when hiring. One important area to cover is employee evaluations. These are useful in determining whether employees are doing their job and how they can improve. You will need to set up a system of when and how to perform these evaluations.

Reporting requirements. How will you keep track of what your employees are doing? You will need to develop a system to track your employees' week-to-week or month-to-month progress on certain jobs. This also provides you with information for your general record keeping files in case of any discrepancy.

Time sheets. How will you require employees to keep records of their time? If you don't have many employees, it doesn't make a lot of sense to use time clocks, but do develop time sheets to keep records of hours worked. The government requires this, as well.

Pay structure. Incorporate the pay structure into job descriptions. Decide how you will determine pay—based on job classification, years of experience, skill level?

Pay periods. Set a policy regarding when and how often you will pay employees.

Benefits structure. As a microbusiness owner, you probably are not in a position to pay benefits. However, you should address certain questions so that you are prepared: What are your own policies on benefits? Do employees need to work for a specified amount of time before they qualify for certain benefits? Will you pay a percentage of certain benefits? You should develop a benefits policy for employees to sign; this furnishes proof that you advised employees of what they can expect.

Dress codes. People take their fashion seriously. Decide what is acceptable to you in terms of appearance on the job, including hair length and attire, and state it clearly to your employees. New legislature is enacted from time to time; make sure you stay abreast of these laws so as not to violate the rights of your employees with illegal demands.

Attendance policies. Clearly state your expectations and the consequences of not meeting them. If, for example, you are going to fire someone for being late five times, that policy needs to have been in writing so that the employee was aware of it.

Vacation structure. Establish guidelines for vacation time off and pay for all employees.

Training. How will you train employees? Each job should have a training procedure and a training schedule, if needed.

Agreements. If you have a particular agreement or contract with an employee, it needs to be spelled out as a part of your employee policy. A non-compete agreement is another you might consider. If your business requires a particular skill or special knowledge, a non-compete agreement will preclude the employee from doing the same business and utilizing knowledge gained from you to compete against you for a reasonable period of time, often two to five years. Be aware that these agreements are not usually enforceable; they often only serve to deter the employee from thinking about competing.

CLIENTS AND CUSTOMERS.
With clients or customers, it is important to clearly spell out your expectations and any limitations you foresee in your interactions with them. Here are some areas to consider:

Customer service. What is your policy on customer service? It is important to analyze how you like to be treated as a customer and then put your own guidelines in writing. Having a written policy will stop people in their tracks when it comes to asking

> # Having a written policy will stop people in their tracks

for certain things. All you need to do is refer back to the policy: "Our policy on that is ...". Think through every aspect of dealing with customer /client–deadlines, advance payments, refund policies and other possible situations.

For customers: What kind of servicing can they expect on a product? Will you give a refund even if the manufacturer advises customers to mail the product to them for refund or exchange? Will service of product be available? What will be the delivery policy?

For clients: To what extent will satisfaction be provided? Will it cost extra after a specified amount of service (e.g., Any corrections beyond three hours will be billed at the regular hourly rate)? Be clear about the charges for services rendered; spell it out in writing.

Shipping and handling. How will you charge for this? Spell it out.

Quality assurance. Will there be guarantees or warranties? What are the details, conditions?

Customer evaluation forms. It helps you to know how the customer or client feels about your product or service. Will you have customer evaluation forms? How will you use them?

Return policies. Will you take merchandise back? Will you give refunds? If so, under what circumstances? Will you make exchanges? Under what circumstances? Set it all down in writing.

Credit policies. If you are to offer credit, be very clear about the terms. Is there a discount if customers pay early? Are there interest rates or late fees if they are not on time with their payments?

Collection procedure. Some policies and procedures are to be shown to customers or others outside of the company and some are internal. Collection procedures, for example, are an internal function. Write down your procedures (e.g., send a letter after 30 days; send a stronger letter after 60 days; make a phone call after 90 days, etc.). Have a clearly stated practice for collecting money owed you, and follow it.

> **...develop a system to track your employees' week-to-week or month-to-month progress on certain jobs.**

VENDORS AND SUPPLIERS.

Developing guidelines for dealing with vendors can make your business run smoother. These guidelines will help by avoiding unauthorized purchases by employees. Make sure that the vendor or supplier understands who has the authority to order for your company. If you are on a credit basis with the vendor, determine the guidelines you will follow in paying him or her. The polices of each vendor should be noted in the file. Possibly each vendor will have different arrangements with you; make sure these arrangements are spelled out for each.

Conclusion

The systems outlined in this chapter are just a few of the variations that can help you to be efficient and profitable. The kind of system used is not as important as whether it will provide you with information/guidelines that allow you to be as productive as possible. As your business grows and changes, you will most likely need to adjust systems to make sure they continue to serve your purpose.

Establishing and utilizing these systems and policies from the very beginning will alleviate many a headache down the road. Be sure to post policies where clients can see them. Have copies available to hand to customers in case of disputes or complaints.

Many small and microbusiness owners question whether they really need to function in such a structured manner. The answer is simple: If you ever want to become a more sophisticated operation and realize the profits of big businesses, you must behave as they do. Think of the phrase, "Fake it until you make it." It's one I have passed on to my clients through many years of consulting, and it works. "Fake it until you make it," means that if you don't have the money, knowledge or experience of the big players, you nevertheless act as if you do. It's behaving a certain way until you believe it yourself—and others will believe right along with you.

PROCEED WITH CAUTION

CHAPTER TEN

Marketing: The Lifeblood of Your Business

The word marketing is often used but not always understood. What exactly is marketing? Its meaning is two-fold: 1) the movement and sale of products and services to consumers and/or clients, and 2) the dissemination of information about your business to potential customers or clients for the purpose of creating a desire to purchase. It encompasses a variety of tasks, but before you do anything, you must take the most critical first step: market research.

Researching Your Market

Conducting research can help to identify your target market—the people or businesses you want to purchase your product or service—and the marketing methods that work for that group. Market research gives you information that will help you make decisions about the startup, growth and continuation of your business.

Researching your market can take many forms, including phone surveys, in-person surveys, focus groups, product testing, examining competition and more. Focus groups can be blind, in which participants don't know which company is sponsoring the discussion. Product testing can include taste tests and other forms of test marketing. It allows a small segment of your intended market to use the product or service in exchange for feedback. After you collect data, you can sort and analyze it in various ways to draw conclusions and make informed decisions about the development of your business.

Unfortunately, professional market research can be very expensive. Unless you have thousands of dollars to spend on a market research firm, you're not likely to get the highest quality results.

However, you can put together your own focus groups or do informal surveys. Either way you go, the results can be invaluable.

The aim of most market research is product feedback and demographical information—age, occupation, income, ethnicity, etc. Demographics help you to pinpoint your target market, a process sometimes likened to putting a puzzle together. The information also could lead you to alter your product or services so that they are more appealing to a particular target market.

Market research also can yield valuable information on competition—either for companies selling similar products or services, or for companies with other products competing for the same target market. To discover what the competition is doing, act as a potential client or customer, or have someone else do that for you. Find out what's going on and use that information to learn as much as you can about your market. Is the market already saturated with similar products or services? Are other businesses doing well selling to that target market? What marketing methods are working for that market? What can you do differently to give yourself an edge in that market?

If your competition already fills the needs of your target market or is having trouble surviving due to a lower demand for the product (service), you'll need to decide if offering your product or service to this target market is a smart move.

Knowing your industry, as discussed in Chapter Nine, can help you understand your market better. When you know your industry and how you fit into it, you'll be better prepared for various kinds of contract opportunities available through the government and larger companies. Good library reference sections have solid business and industry information, especially at the libraries of universities with strong business programs. Another good resource is associations, which often keep statistics and can provide up-to-date information. Trade journals do the same and offer invaluable industry news. Before you can make sound decisions about your target market, you need this kind of solid information.

Industry trends will influence your marketing decisions. Knowing the latest trend gives you an opportunity to stay on top of and in front of upcoming trends. Riding the crest of the trend, you're likely to make more money than the person who is not in tune.

EXAMPLE: *A female surfer in Southern California noticed a steadily increasing number of women and girls in the ocean over previous years. She also knew from personal experience how difficult it was to find equipment and clothing tailored for females in traditional surf shops. She opened the first women's surf shop in the area. Within the first three months of operation, her shop was doing a booming business. She saw that trend coming and is riding the wave of prosperity.*

EXAMPLE: *On a larger scale, a current national trend positively impacts microbusiness development. The whole country is changing, making a 180-degree turn compared to how it was 40 or 50 years ago, when large corporations were the lifeblood of the country. With the downsizing of corporations to compete with smaller companies, the trend is that by the year 2000, businesses with fewer than 50 employees will generate 80 percent of all jobs in this country. Small businesses, with microbusinesses included, will be the backbone of this nation for many years to come.*

Many people will be forced by downsizing to create their own jobs. By so doing, they often move into territory that is foreign to them. This creates another trend, an increased need for agencies and individuals skilled enough to guide prospective and current business owners through the process of starting and running an effective and profitable business.

Proper research of your market will better prepare you to take advantage of opportunities as they present themselves. It will help you to identify these opportunities before they become apparent to the general public.

Many people will be forced by downsizing to create their own jobs.

The Four "Ps" of Marketing

Once you're solidly committed to a market and an industry, you'll need to actually market your product or service. Pay attention to the following Ps when doing your marketing—not just one, but all of them. To be successful, you'll need all of them in place.

PRODUCT. If you've done your market research, you'll have a good idea of what product or service you will offer. It must be something many people will pay to have.

PLACE. This is where you will operate. Effective marketing makes the product or service accessible to the market. In retail, location is critical. For example, if your retail operation sits off the street or in an alley, with no signage on the main thoroughfare, your product is not accessible to your marketplace. It is highly unlikely that you'll get customers into your store without a huge amount of word-of-mouth marketing (which you can't control), advertising with specific directions or better signage.

PRICE. Just like the Northwestern University microbusiness training program, in which the price prevented many from signing up, your product or service must be priced according to what your market will bear.

PROMOTION. To sell, you've got to let people know you exist and that you have a terrific product or service at a reasonable price. There are hundreds of ways to do that. Below are 22 of the most effective marketing methods.

Twenty-Two Marketing Ideas

Effective marketing requires at least three different approaches in play at any given time–five are even more beneficial. For example, you might network several times a month with different groups, regularly distribute letters or postcards and follow up with a phone call. Collectively, you have three different methods going at one time. Distributing business cards as you meet people is a fourth way.

Vary your methods from time to time to test which are most effective. Also, adjust your printed materials periodically to add new information or to give them a more current look.

1. BUSINESS CARDS/LETTERHEAD. Business cards and letterhead are often the first image of your business that people will see–a snapshot of your business that leaves an impression. They are the lead figures in a list of items that projects your business to the public. Collectively called collateral material, those items include business cards, letterhead, brochures, catalog sheets, point-of-purchase materials, displays, banners, posters, headers and tags. They are among the most important components of business image.

With your logo and company name on them, business cards present a snapshot of your business image. Even if you operate a business from your bedroom in your pajamas, people will never suspect that as long as you project a professional image. They'll be more concerned with what you can do for them. If your business cards are appealing, people will think more highly of you as a provider. If not done well, they can actually turn people off, often without you ever realizing it. Letterhead, envelopes and business cards are usually printed at the same time, using the same logo, tagline, colors, paperstock and ink. All information provided in this section applies equally to letterhead, envelopes and business cards.

What makes a business card memorable is a clean, crisp look with appropriate use of color. Color provides a powerful attraction to your card and, consequently, to your business. When deciding on color, think not only in terms of ink but of paper stock. For example, two ink colors on colored paper effectively gives you three colors.

The more color on your collateral material, the more people are likely to remember you and what you do. Be careful to choose colors that are easy to read; a light gray ink, for example, is often difficult to see, especially in a small font. Remember that small type is hard on the eyes. If people can't easily read your card, they are not likely to call for your product (service).

Pay special attention not to clutter up your business card. In addition to your business name and logo, it should list your name, address, phone number, fax number, and e-mail and Web site addresses, if you have them. Too much on the front distracts the eye and puts people off, often causing them not to read it. If you feel the need to put lots of information on your business card, consider printing on both sides or having a folded card that opens.

A note to home-based businesses: Many who work from home do not want the public to know their home address, so they print no address on the card. This is a sure sign that you do work from home and that you have not taken the necessary steps to present a professional image. Instead, consider renting a post office box that allows you to use its street address and a suite number that is actually your box number. Franchises such as Mail Boxes, Etc. and Postal Annex, as well as smaller local operations, will allow you to do this. This gives you a more professional image. While I don't encourage using post office boxes on business cards (e.g. P.O. Box 1234), it has become a more accepted practice.

Another alternative to using your home address is to obtain access to an executive suite. Some executive suites will charge you to use their address just for mail delivery. They will then either forward your mail to you or allow you to pick it up. For home-based business owners who need to meet with clients outside of their homes, some executive suites will rent conference rooms on an as-needed basis. You pay hourly for the time used per month. Don't be afraid to negotiate a deal. Remember to ASK for what you want!

Letterhead. Letterhead, envelopes and business cards are usually printed at the same time, using the same logo, tagline and colors; paperstock and ink. All information provided in this section applies equally to letterhead, envelopes and business cards.

2. BROCHURES. A brochure has a specific purpose: to entice the reader to want to know more about your business. It usually tells who you are, what you do, for whom you do it and something about the owner(s).

The idea is to get the reader to call you for more information about your business. That way, you have an opportunity to dis-

cuss your business in more detail and to learn how you can serve that reader's needs. It becomes your selling opportunity. The key, then, is to fashion the brochure so that it provides good information but leaves a few questions unanswered. For example, a brochure should not provide pricing information, estimates or specifics about your work.

Keep your brochure simple but appealing. Don't clutter it with lots of pictures and words. Take a hint from professional graphic designers and be mindful of the "sacredness" of white space—areas without words or artwork. White space is a design element interspersed throughout the brochure, along with text and art, to give a sense of openness and to make reading easier.

You can add white space to a brochure by using headings and lists (such as bullet points), instead of long, detailed narratives. Of course, some narrative is necessary, at the very least to describe your company (or you) and its philosophy or mission statement. If you need to write more about some items or put a lot of information in the brochure, make sure that it is appealing to the eye. Box it or change the format so that it isn't plain or boring. Use graphics for eye appeal, including lines to divide sections. It is acceptable to put a client list on your material, just be sure not to violate the confidentiality of any client.

Make your brochures colorful, if possible, using the same ink and paper colors as for your business card and letterhead. Your logo also should be prominent. It's important to present a consistent image to the public so that people begin to associate your logo and colors with your business and products or services. With so much printed brochure paper, card stock and postcard stock available today, low-cost brochures and business cards are becoming increasingly acceptable.

3. CATALOG SHEETS. Catalog sheets are an inexpensive (compared to other forms of advertising) way to display products and distribute information about the products you sell. These are sheets displaying items you have for sale. They are used when you don't have enough items to fill a complete catalog. Catalog sheets can be expensive; however, by carefully researching local printers, you can find discounted rates, especially if you search for those that exclusively do catalogs. Specialized printers can make catalog sheets affordable even for a microbusiness owner.

When designing a catalog sheet, make sure it's not cluttered with too many items on one page. Layout is critical because you want the public to be drawn to it, not repelled or distracted by it. If you design your own catalog sheets, make sure you put a stock number and adequate description for each item. While you may give pricing information on the catalog sheets, it's a good idea to produce a separate pricing sheet when prices are subject to change. Buying in quantity, which reduces costs, raises the chance that prices will change before you run out of sheets.

To cut down on cost, print a price sheet from your computer, make copies at a local copy shop (black ink, regular paper) and attach it to your color catalog sheets. It's also possible to produce attractive line drawings of products and to print in two colors, rather than in four-color. Just make sure the final product doesn't look cheap.

4. POINT-OF-PURCHASE DISPLAYS, TAGS, HEADERS. These are low-cost items that draw attention to your products when they're on display in stores or elsewhere. Take great care when developing these items. Use your logo and make sure to project an image that is consistent throughout all your materials in the public eye. Color is again an important consideration. A graphic artist can help you develop these items.

5. BANNERS AND POSTERS. The same applies here. Project an image that is consistent throughout all of the materials that you have out in the public.

6. CUSTOMER EVALUATIONS. Evaluations offer a tremendous opportunity to determine whether your customers are pleased with your product or service. Evaluations let them know that their opinions count and allow you to understand how you might better serve that customer or client. Suggestions for better customer service and for new customer polices and procedures can result from evaluations.

The evaluation should be a simple questionnaire that you mail after providing the service or hand to the customer with the product. The idea is for them to complete the form and return it to you. The evaluation can also double as a market survey when you ask for pertinent data, such as age, income, occupation, etc.

7. INTERNET. The Internet and the World Wide Web are fast becoming tremendous marketing vehicles for businesses of any size. While the most successful Web marketers are those with products to sell to a very specific target market, there is growth and opportunity for most kinds of businesses.

Remember these points about marketing on the Internet:

- **Don't leave the same advertisement on your Web site for more than two weeks. Switch products or emphasize a different service to keep attracting people to the site. Also, be sure to have a picture of a product on your Web page, if you are marketing products.**

- **Provide a way for those visiting your site to purchase the product.**

- **Indicate whether you accept credit cards. (It's a good idea to do so, for credit cards are the fastest way for people to buy goods.)**

- **Provide an address and/or phone number—preferably an 800 number—if you are selling a service.**

- **Be as descriptive as possible while being succinct.**

8. NETWORKING. For microbusiness owners, networking is probably the most effective way to market a business. Networking happens in all sorts of situations, not just organized meetings. Whenever you ask about someone's business and tell about yours, you are networking.

For those gatherings specifically geared toward networking, here are a few tips:

- Set an objective before the event, such as a specific number of contacts you want to establish at that function.

- Focus on working, not schmoozing. Don't stay in conversations with the same individual for long periods of time. Excuse yourself and move on to speak with others.

- Always seek prospects who might be interested in your product or service. Find ways to assess their potential as a customer (client). When you meet other business owners, consider whether a strategic alliance is possible, allowing you to work on a project together. Don't overlook an opportunity to create win/win situations.

As a microbusiness whose target market is business owners, be careful not to network with only small or new businesses. They often work on a shoestring budget (as you might!) and may be unable to afford your product or service. Networking with them exclusively will not move you forward. Identify and begin to interact with those who can afford what you have to sell, even if it means going beyond your comfort level.

Also be careful about joining organizations that expect attendance at monthly meetings. Why? Because you see the same people month after month without expanding your networking circle or generating additional revenues for your business. It is true that the better people know you, the more likely they are to do business with you. Just don't limit yourself to the same small group of prospects.

To avoid meeting the same people time after time, go to different networking groups. Limit meetings with the same group to about three. Choose carefully the groups you join. If you decide to join a group, join just one. Even networking in two or three different circles may bring you into contact with some of the same people. Though they may have no need for your product or service themselves, they often will refer others to your business if they feel comfortable with you.

Though networking is relatively inexpensive, it does cost money. The expense is generally well justified, particularly if you go to a function attended by individuals in your target market. Networking is such a critical part of marketing for microbusinesses that you should allocate money every month to attend at least two separate networking events. Deduct the cost from your marketing budget.

9. FOCUS GROUPS. Widely used as market research, focus groups are generally groups of eight to 12 people who talk about a specific subject under the direction of a professional facilitator. The purpose of the focus group is to preview a product or service and get feedback from the potential target market.

Screened participants usually fall into a category pertinent to the company conducting the group. For example, if you're trying to sell dog food, you would want dog owners in that focus group. If you're trying to sell jewelry, you probably would want women in that group. The facilitator usually has a written script, and sessions often are videotaped. The company sponsoring the group normally has access to view the group in session through a one-way window.

For the data to be considered scientific, you must compare the discussions of a number of groups. As a microbusiness owner, it's not likely that you can afford to pay for professionally administered focus groups. But consider asking groups of individuals—members of your networking groups or people from specific organizations—to participate in an informal discussion of your product or service. Use the five points of asking to find groups willing to sit down and have a discussion. If you want to include certain types of people, such as professionals of a certain income level, think in terms of professional groups and organizations that cater to those types of people. For example, if you need feedback from battered women, contact a YWCA with a battered women's facility or another non-profit organization that provides shelter to battered women.

Have someone knowledgeable help you analyze the data you collect from a focus group. The data may relate to marketing or to improving your product or service.

Normally, individuals who attend focus groups are paid $35 to $75 for the time they spend discussing your product or service. Make it clear ahead of time if no fee will be paid. Consider having refreshments available for those participating.

Though focus groups take a lot of time to coordinate, they are an excellent way to determine whether your product or service has a chance in the marketplace. If you are daring enough to attempt it, you probably will be able to get decent results. Use these groups for feedback on new products or services you wish to offer or to test a concept to determine if it should be developed further.

10. EVENT SPONSORSHIP. Public relations—how the general public perceives what you are doing—is the single most important way to establish a positive and professional image for your business. Associating your name with a worthy cause is one way to cultivate a good public image. Just be sure that when you sponsor or cosponsor an event—giving up your time, money, products or services—you get something in return. The rewards need not be monetary; exposure and recognition in the public eye can be equally valuable.

When you sponsor an event, don't be shy about getting publicity for it. Ask television/radio stations and newspapers to interview you about it. Think up story ideas about the event to pitch to them. Make sure your name is on every piece of written material about the event and spoken at every mention of the event.

11. PRESS RELEASES. Press releases are announcements that you send to newspapers, magazines, television/radio stations and any other group you wish to notify. If you want news organizations to cover an activity, send a short letter along with the press release asking for coverage. Press releases can cover a variety of topics. They can:

- **Introduce new services,**
- **Announce an award,**
- **Predict trends in your community or industry,**
- **Announce an event, activity, class, appearance,**
- **Announce a new contract,**
- **Offer unusual services,**
- **Announce milestones,**
- **Introduce new management,**
- **Announce shop opening.**

There is no guarantee that any organization will publish the press release, but it stands a better chance if it is well-written, relevant and accompanied by a photo. Photographs take up space in newspapers, show that you are real and capture readers by providing a visual attraction. And television stations are more apt to select a story that has visual appeal. Make sure the photo is an action shot, not a head shot, and that photographic quality is high.

Call your local library's reference desk to get a list of news organizations in your city. Be aware, though, that the library's lists may not be up to date. Bookstores often carry publications of news organizations. Or contact the Chamber of Commerce.

Send your press release at least three weeks before the event to all the community papers, as smaller publications are more likely to run press releases. Send it also to television and appropriate radio stations, as well as to your city's major daily news- paper. If the larger news organizations consider it interesting enough, they will assign a reporter to the story. Many cities have some kind of daily or weekly business newspaper, as well, which often will publish your press release and may even write a larger story.

Press Release Tips

Release time/contact person: This information goes at the very top of a press release. Put either "For immediate release" or an effective release date at top left. A contact name, with phone number, goes top right for easy access.

HEADLINE. Located just below the release time and contact person, the headline should pull the reader in so that he or she wants to read it. Make a bold statement that will grab the reader's attention, but pertinent and factual as well.

FIRST PARAGRAPH. Often the only thing assignment editors read, the first paragraph must answer the questions: who, what, when, where, why and how.

SECOND PARAGRAPH. Expound a little on the subject of the press release.

THIRD PARAGRAPH. Mention your name, your company, what you do and what your relationship is to the event (e.g., event sponsor).

FINAL PARAGRAPH. Wrap it up with any other pertinent information about the event. End the press release with either "-30-" or "# # #" across the bottom center. The entire release should not be more than a page and a half, double-spaced (preferably one page). See the sample in the appendix.

12. SPEECHES. Another public relations enhancer is to make speeches. Many organizations are hungry for speakers. Start with local service groups, such as Kiwanis, Rotary or Lions Club, which generally meet on a weekly basis and are always looking for speakers. Use your presentation as an opportunity to educate people about your product or service without making it a total commercial. Include your product, book, booklets, etc., as props for your speech, so that you are not overtly trying to sell them. Brochures can serve the same purpose, if you provide a service. Refer to them several times during the presentation.

Speaking before service organizations can give you valuable practice and boost your confidence. If you network effectively, you also begin to make connections; membership often includes key business people, politicians and professionals of all levels. Eventually, you will move on to speak to organizations more specifically targeted to your market. At some point, you may want to begin to charge for your talks, especially if you motivate, stimulate or educate the audience.

13. CLASSES, WORKSHOPS OR SEMINARS. To become known as an authority in your field, teach a class. It adds to your credibility, looks great on your resume or other credentials, and gives you an opportunity to market your product or service. (You can even make a little money doing it.) Once you're an established authority, you can market yourself to television/radio stations and newspapers as someone to call on when they need an expert in that field.

Some of your options for teaching are: the Learning Annex, or a similar seminar-based program in your community; community colleges; nonprofit centers; and associations. You can also offer a workshop in conjunction with a lecture you give. If you anticipate high revenues for a seminar, try sponsoring and organizing it yourself, using a meeting room in a local hotel or convention center. Be aware, however, that you bear the burden of all costs associated with the seminar when you host it.

14. ARTICLES. Writing articles is another way to establish yourself as an authority on a subject and gain valuable exposure for yourself and your product or service. It also allows you to call yourself a published author, which enhances your credentials. To successfully employ this marketing method, you need to be a good writer. If you're not, try hiring a professional writer to ghostwrite for you or to edit what you've written.

Your first step in writing articles is to decide on your topic. Then research which publications (magazines, newspapers or newsletters) might take an interest in your subject. Think in terms of industry publications, trade journals and general interest publications with "departments" related to your topic. You can also start with the publication and research what kinds of articles it takes, then gear your story toward that.

An invaluable resource for finding a venue in which to publish your work is the *Writer's Market*. Writer's Digest Books publishes a current issue every year filled with thousands of publisher listings, including contact names, addresses, and submission and editorial requirements. The book also lists tips from editors, as well as practical advice on query letters, manuscript mechanics, unsolicited manuscripts and more. I recommend it highly.

Try to find a publication for which you can write consistently, including community newspapers or local publications, even though they might be obscure. Often such publications don't pay, or pay very little. But the objective here is to market yourself and become published, not to be paid. Charge the cost of doing it to marketing expense.

15. TV OR RADIO GUEST APPEARANCE. Television is a powerful medium. Take any opportunity you have to publicize your company. Better yet, make an opportunity to appear on TV or on radio to:

- **Introduce a product or service that is new and different,**
- **Talk about the activity you are sponsoring,**
- **Preview the program you've developed or the book you've written,**
- **Demonstrate a technique,**
- **Educate viewers/listeners about a subject in which you're an expert.**

To be a guest on TV or radio, contact the station or the producer of the show you want to be on. Give at least three weeks' notice but no more than four. Offer several dates and times you are available to have a better chance of being chosen. In other words, be flexible. And don't stop with just one station or show. Send your query letters to several different programs. Doing so increases your possibilities of being asked to speak on one of them.

If you have a product that the general public might find interesting, for example, dried floral arrangements, you can demonstrate the process and market your business. Try the local morning news programs, weekend morning news spots, or talk shows produced at local television stations. The Christmas holidays would be an excellent time for such a demonstration.

For radio programs, it is important to remember that the audience cannot see you. Speak clearly and in terms easily understood. It's hard to promote a product on the air unless you can be very descriptive of it and give suggestions about where the audience might see it. For example, if your product is on a Web site, refer to it on the show so that people can view the product on their computers.

Whether you're on TV or radio, come prepared with points you want to make and answers to anticipated questions. Try to direct the interviewer's attention to areas you want to address. There are several ways of doing this:

- **Make arrangements to meet and talk with the interviewer prior to the show.**
- **Hand a list of questions and/or interest areas to the interviewer prior to going on air.**
- **Send information to the producer a few days before the show.**

Be prepared to answer questions succinctly so that the listening audience clearly understands what you have to say. Call-in shows are especially fun, but be prepared for all kinds of weird questions and comments. Keep your cool.

16. YELLOW PAGES. A Yellow Pages listing doesn't cost a thing, but placing an ad in the Yellow Pages can be expensive. As a microbusiness, where every dollar is precious, it's especially important to estimate how much you expect to gain from a Yellow Pages ad before purchasing one, and to monitor it closely if you do.

First, gauge whether most people would be inclined to look in the Yellow Pages to find you. If you're an artist or a public speaker, or if you sell cremation urns, it's not likely that you'll get a large response from the Yellow Pages. On the other hand, if you offer secretarial services, a Yellow Pages ad might be of benefit. You'll compete with others listed, but if your ad is catchy, you might draw some customers.

If you decide to place an ad, first choose a small, plain one to test the feasibility. Explore categories carefully to determine which is the most suitable for your ad. Track the results of your ad carefully to calculate your return. Every time a new prospect calls, ask the question, "How did you hear about us?" Analyze your data to determine whether the Yellow Pages ad brings in enough revenue to cover its cost and add to revenue. You should see a return of at least 20 percent over the cost of the ad. If you're not seeing that, don't waste your time and money to advertise in the Yellow Pages.

17. LETTERS/POSTCARDS. For microbusinesses, letters and postcards can be one of the most effective and least expensive ways to keep your name in front of prospective customers and to obtain appointments to meet in person. The key to this method is to carefully select your recipients.

Mailing Strategy. In mass mailings, numbers count. Statistics indicate that 1/2 to 2 percent return on direct mail pieces is the norm. In fact, a 2 percent response rate is good. For example, if 2 percent respond on a 500-piece mailing, that's only 10 responses. And 10 responses does not mean 10 sales.

On the other hand, if you can afford to send out 2,000 pieces in a mailing and get a 2 percent return, that's 40 responses. Turning at least half of those into orders or sales could prove worthwhile, depending on the cost of your product. But if you have only a small number of people to mail to, your anticipated return will not be great. Before you decide on a mass mailing, look carefully at the cost of postage and paper, and at your preparation time. Do the numbers to determine whether it makes sense for you to use mass mailing to market your business.

To achieve a better response rate, consider doing your mailing differently. Instead of mailing 2,000 pieces at a time, break it down. Send out only 10 letters a week, keeping a list of your mailing (contact name, date mailed, etc.). Follow up by phone within three days to find out if:

- **The contacts received your information,**

- **They have any questions,**

- **You can meet with them in person to discuss your service or product.**

Note for your records whatever occurs with the call (e.g., call back in three weeks, never got the person, send brochure). This gives you a master file with all the action taken–when you sent the letter, when you spoke with the contacts, their response, follow-up action needed, etc.

Your overall strategy, then, might look something like this:

1. Send out 10 pieces a week.

2. Follow up with a phone call within three days.

3. Within 10 more days, follow up the phone call with a different mailing piece (no more than 3 pieces per business or individual in succession).

4. Repeat the cycle for 10 more pieces.

Follow-up might include a thank-you note for taking the time to speak with you, directed either to the secretary or individual with whom you spoke.

Marketing letter specifics. Marketing letters can be tricky since business owners receive letters every day. Your letter needs to stand out. It's a good idea to develop a standard marketing letter that is interesting and draws people into it. Address the envelope to a specific individual, and enclose the standard letter.

Put a bold heading at the top—something that attracts the reader immediately. It can raise a question or make a statement followed by an exclamation mark. Leave lots of white space on the page so that it's not solid narrative. There should be some bulleted points and/or some headings in different fonts, type styles and/or point sizes.

When you find a combination that works, stick with it. Psychologists tell us that people must hear or see your name seven times before it begins to register. This is why it's important to send out smaller groupings of mail and do your follow-up work. You get a pattern going; the person begins to see your name a number of times, even if it is just on the phone message that a secretary or assistant writes. It all works to help you market yourself.

Postcard specifics. Postcards are a good follow-up to your first marketing letter. Plus, they often allow you to be more personal, even playful. Take care, though, to present yourself well on the postcard. You might have the best product or service, but if it is not presented in an appealing, acceptable manner, chances are you won't get very far.

The key here is whether the postcard is visually appealing. How do you do that? With effective use of color, with pictures of your products, with a nice verse or description of the services you offer, with a pleasing layout, with colors, dark enough ink and readable type.

18. FLYERS. Use flyers in much the same way as marketing letters and postcards, though flyers normally announce an event, program or activity with a specific date and time. Flyers give you an opportunity to use a different vehicle to serve the same purpose. They're also more versatile. You can hand out flyers at activities, post them in different areas, give them to organizations to distribute to their membership and more.

Placement of information on a flyer determines how effective it will be. Emphasize information the same as with marketing letters, by point size, type style and different fonts. Words placed in eye-catching ways, on angles, in arches or in a circular pattern are effective. Graphics serve a similar purpose. Use color whenever possible.

19. BILLBOARDS. Microbusinesses seem to forget this great opportunity to gain recognition and customers. Billboards are relatively inexpensive, and their cost is far more justifiable than money spent on Yellow Pages ads. For one, billboards normally charge by the month, so you can test your response for a month before committing to more time. You can't do that with the Yellow Pages.

Billboards include signs on bus benches, buses themselves, cabs, buildings, stand-alone billboards and billboards atop buildings. They're often visible from a highway or main thoroughfare; these are the best spots. A billboard's size and location gives it a tremendous impact. People driving past a particular billboard every day for a month may see it 40 times or more. You can bet they will remember your name, particularly if you have a catchy phrase on the billboard. A phone number with a name as part of it, makes it easier to remember (e.g., 555-DOGS or 1-800-VISA-YES).

Don't expect immediate sales from a billboard, whose main purpose is impact and awareness. In fact, it's best to use billboard advertising in conjunction with another medium, such as flyers, media advertising or public relations.

Investigate billboards in your area. Sometimes you can rent them for as little as $200 a month, which is exceedingly reasonable. I've even seen them for as little as $50+ per month, plus the cost of the posted piece. It depends on your city and how many billboard companies compete there. Some cities have ordinances banning billboards from certain parts of town. Find out where the billboards are, who operates them and what the rates are.

Try it for a month and see whether it works for you. Though advertising generally must be consistent to work, billboards can work even on a sporadic basis. Consider renting a billboard for one or two months during a peak period. For example, if you have an item that's especially popular around the holidays, advertise just for the month of November or for November and December. You probably will get a good return on your investment.

20. EXHIBITS. Exhibits can be as simple as placing materials or products on a table at a networking function or as elaborate as a professional trade show display. While most microbusinesses cannot afford full-blown trade shows, they can take advantage of smaller, more affordable opportunities to exhibit their products or services, such as at monthly association meetings, conferences, workshops and seminars that allow exhibits.

Expositions (expos) are another place to exhibit, whether they be expos for small business, women or minority-owned business, or business-to-business expos. Expos and other such shows allow owners to display services and products at a booth in a large exhibit hall. To rent a booth costs anywhere from $50 to several thousand dollars.

Deciding Whether to Exhibit. The main question to ask yourself before spending money to exhibit is whether you will benefit. The general rule of thumb is this: If the leads you generate from the expo will eventually earn you 20 percent to 40 percent over your costs, then it makes sense to do it. Decide whether you should exhibit by answering these questions:

- **How many people are expected? On average, you can anticipate talking to no more than 20 percent of those in attendance.**

- **What kind of people are expected? How many will be people in your target market?**

- **How much does it cost to exhibit?**

EXAMPLE: *You are a bridal consultant and there is a bridal expo once a year in your area. Hundreds of companies and individuals who provide products and services to the bridal market will have booths there. Of the 1,000 people expected to attend, you can anticipate talking to no more than 200. You probably won't make sales on the spot, but can generate enough leads for sales in the near future. Of the 200 you talk to, with luck 20 will become solid leads. Even if only 10 people were interested, it might still be worthwhile for you to participate, depending on the cost of your product or service. Suppose a booth costs $2,000. If those 10-20 leads can generate $2,400 to $2,800, then the expo may be beneficial.*

Exhibit Tips. Don't attempt to set up for an exhibit alone. You want to have at least one other person in the booth with you so that you don't miss opportunities to draw people in to show them what you have. While one person is talking with someone, the other person can pass out materials or engage others walking by. You have a greater chance to generate the kind of leads you need by having two people present in the booth at all times.

In your booth, be sure to have some manner of obtaining mailing information—whether it's a straightforward sign-up sheet for your mailing list, individual index cards or a drawing that entices people to drop a business card in a fishbowl. (If you promise to give something away, then follow through and do it.) Take the time to make the sign-up sheet attractive; print it on the computer. Leave space for name, address, zip code and phone numbers. The zip code is important; without it, mail often doesn't get to its intended destination.

Remember that it is your responsibility to invite people walking through an exhibit area to stop by your booth. Be the one to engage them in conversation, to present your material and information to them. Don't stand there like a bump on a log and expect them to stop and ask you questions just because you have the best product or service. It's not going to happen.

Follow Up. Make sure you follow up on your efforts to collect the names and phone numbers of individuals passing through the exhibit. Develop a letter or contact form, and send it out within two weeks of the exhibit. Let them know that you appreciated them stopping by your booth. Invite them to meet with you to further discuss what you can offer them, or invite them to another activity (networking, workshop, training, sale, etc. you might be associated with). Use the opportunity to send them information about your business that they may not have already picked up.

Staying in touch is a critical part of building relationships with potential clients or customers. While they themselves may not want what you have to offer, they will pass along your name to friends who do if you establish good rapport and stay in touch with them.

Exhibits can pay off—though not always immediately. They are an opportunity to market, which doesn't always mean making a sale, but does mean disseminating information and establishing relationships. Often you have to go the distance and wait a while before your marketing effort actually pays off. Don't be impatient, just persistent and consistent!

21. ADVERTISING. Microbusiness owners often do not have the capital to advertise effectively. Yet sometimes advertising is necessary to generate revenue. Keep in mind that advertising pays only if it is repetitive and broad-based. Advertising in one issue of a magazine or in one newspaper edition is like pouring money down the drain. People must see your name or business name at least seven times to remember who you are and what you do.

If you feel you must advertise to get clients or customers, here are some guidelines to follow as you research the possibilities:

- Prepare an advertising budget for a full year.

- Look for ways to make the available funds go as far as possible.

- Determine circulation/exposure rates for all methods you consider.

- Determine how much of the "audience" falls into your target market.

- Exhaust alternatives—letters, postcards, networking, follow-up phone calls, etc.—before you spend money on advertising.

- Try advertising in a directory before you spend on spot advertising. A directory listing or special-edition ad is likely to be viewed more often than a single-issue ad.

- Be consistent once you decide to advertise. Use multiple exposure of various media to be effective.

- Don't expect an immediate onslaught of sales. Hopefully you will generate some interest. But then you have to close the sale.

Once you decide to advertise, spend the money to have your ads professionally done. Don't waste your money with an ineffective ad. It's a good idea to test the waters to be sure an ad will work. Be methodical in your approach. Gather some associates for a discussion group, and present samples of several well-crafted ads. Get their opinion on which ad is most effective.

Use two or more small groups, if possible. Weigh the feedback and decide on the ad or, if necessary, develop another.

Whatever you do, don't let anyone talk you into a long contract or a bigger ad than you can afford—or an ad at all, if you're not sure this is the right thing to do. Additionally, don't let someone else's deadline push you. If you are not totally comfortable with all aspects of the proposition, don't do it. Another offer will come right behind the first one. A good habit is always to take a day to make a decision.

22. CERTIFICATION AS MBE/WBE/DBE. These three acronyms stand for business enterprises owned by people who are members of an ethnic minority, women or are disadvantaged in some way (e.g. blind, low income). Being certified as a business owner belonging to one of these groups gives you special opportunities to contract with the government, whether at the city, county, state or federal level. Contracting with these agencies gives you the opportunity to gain knowledge and dollars, and to advance your business much further and faster than without it.

In most states there is an agency that handles business certification for the state. It might be the Department of Trans- portation, Department of Commerce or some other; usually major cities have departments that issue certification packages and pass on completed forms to the certifying agency within that state. To become certified, you must provide documentation substantiating that your business is minority- or female-owned and/or that you have generated revenues less than a certain amount (usually $2 million a year) to be considered a disadvantaged business enterprise.

Often temporary certification is issued while processing takes place, if all documentation is submitted. Most municipalities (states, cities, counties, authorities, federal, etc.) have guidelines stipulating that a percentage of all contracts must have minority, disadvantaged and female business participation on them. This guideline opens up opportunities, for microbusinesses in particular, to compete for sometimes big-dollar contracts. Certification must be renewed annually.

A word of advice: Never rely on the government as your company's sole source of revenue. Rather than look at a government contract as the meat and potatoes, look at it as gravy for your business. Always have something else going that will bring in enough revenue to sustain your operation.

If you pursue contracts with the government at any level, understand what to expect. Read the regulations and guidelines referred to in the request for bids to know how to bid effectively. To see such regulations, contact the government office issuing the bid request.

The Freedom of Information Act requires all levels of government to disclose certain information to you upon request. Find out which companies have bid on these contracts in the past. How much did they bid? Who was awarded the bid and what was the total award amount? Did that company come in under or over the bid? Was the work satisfactory? Often you will have to make a written request for such information. State that the request is under the Freedom of Information Act and the government agency is obliged to provide the information to you. Always inquire as to how long it will take for the response, as it will vary.

Don't make the mistake of thinking that the government has no need for your product or service. In one instance, a clown secured a contract with the USO (United Services Organization) to entertain military troops in his area. Who would have thought that there would be a government contract available for clowns? Whatever you have to offer, you can bet that the government will buy it at some point in time.

Cities will often have contracting assistance centers, such as the federally subsidized Procurement Assistance Centers, or PACs. These centers often have up-to-date computer listings of available contracts.

Never rely on the government as your company's sole source of revenue.

When contracting with the government at any level, don't fall prey to the "low bid syndrome." Most agencies looking to contract a job already know what it will cost to do it. Normally, they have a "responsible range" for the bid. If yours is the low bid but it falls below the responsible range, you will not get the contract. The government concern in such a case would be that you have not calculated your bid properly and, therefore, might not complete the contract due to financial shortfalls.

On government or any other contracts, make sure you do a cost analysis to determine your direct and indirect expenses. Cover all your overhead expenses and always calculate a profit. If you feel the bid is too high, find ways to cut expenses but maintain a profit margin. When calculated properly, government contracts can provide a degree of security, especially if it is a large contract. Again, be sure to maintain other work or good levels of operating capital so that you don't get into a cash-flow bind waiting for your checks.

Aside from contracting with the government, certification is also useful in contracting with large corporations. Even with affirmative action under scrutiny, most larger companies maintain goals for minority and female participation as vendors. Frequently, certification is required just as a convenience (so they know a business is legitimately female, minority or disadvantaged) to the corporation. A corporation will honor your certification by a state or local municipality.

The bidding process with corporations is not usually as tedious as with government agencies, but proposals usually are required. Many such contracts will be multiyear on an as-needed basis. In other words, the corporation can call on you for a product or service whenever it wants, over a period of time. Ideally, you would have a consumable or disposable product that requires frequent replenishing.

Purchasing councils, which exist in most major cities, are another entity that may require certification. Individual councils gear themselves toward minority, women or small-business vendors. These purchasing councils usually are operated as nonprofit corporations and charge a membership fee to both kinds of members: small business owners wanting to market themselves and larger corporations looking for vendors of products or services. Corporate members of a purchasing council (sometimes called different names) often will purchase only from small business members of that council. If you seek to join a purchasing council, expect to meet eligibility guidelines to become certified, if you are not already certified. Different criteria exist for different councils.

Public Relations vs. Advertising

Public relations or advertising—which works better? It's a common question in business. For microbusinesses, the answer is simple: In cost and in effectiveness, there is no comparison to good public relations.

It's true that with advertising, you have more control. You decide where to place your ad and how it will look. And because you pay for it, you can be certain your message will be transmitted. With public relations, there is no guarantee that a publica- tion, television or radio station will transmit your message at all.

CAUTION

SLIPPERY WHEN WET

But the cost of advertising done properly—that is, consistently and broadly based—far outweighs the benefit of greater control. Microbusinesses need to focus on ways to market that do not cost a lot of money. Public relations is much less expensive than advertising. It can even be more effective, if you work smart and constantly look for exposure opportunities. Here are two examples of how public relations can outpace advertising.

EXAMPLE: *Several years ago, I was responsible for marketing a microbusiness training program sponsored by the city of Chicago. Ten different organizations were to provide training to specific geographic areas of the city. My area covered three zip codes on the west side. I wrote a press release and included in it a picture of me and the coordinator of the college that was cosponsoring this particular training program. An ethnic-oriented daily newspaper printed my* *press release and the picture. In the same issue appeared a paid advertisement—about an eighth of a page, a decent sized ad—for a similar program offered by a different organization for a different geographic area. The ad had no graphics and no picture, just copy. It was not poorly done, but it had no visuals at all. I got tremendous response to my press release—so much so that people from the geographic area served by the other organization responded to my article instead, not having seen the ad at all. My press release took up three times the space of the ad, with the picture alone about the same size as the ad. People were drawn to the headline, to the picture and to the story in general. Far more people responded to the press release than to the ad. The other organization paid more than $1,000 for the ad and got nowhere near the results that I did for just the cost of the picture.*

EXAMPLE: *In January 1996, San Diego's major daily newspaper featured an article on the Women's Business Training Center. It ran on the front page of the features section. Seven months later, I had received more than 300 responses to the article and more were still coming in. An advertisement that took about a quarter of the space the article did and ran in the same paper at a similar time, got only five responses.*

This is not to say that you shouldn't advertise, just that advertising need not be synonymous with marketing. Advertising is only one form of marketing, as is public relations. Never rely on just one or the other to bring you clients or customers. Combine either of them with at least two other strategies for effective marketing.

And certainly, there are many more ways to market than mentioned in this chapter. Don't limit your possibilities. Just make sure that the methods are sound, will give you good results and are affordable.

SECTION III

● **MAPPING YOUR JOURNEY**

CHAPTER ELEVEN

Strategic Planning

I often ask clients if they would go to the airport, bus terminal or train station and ask for a ticket on the next thing moving without knowing; exactly where they are going, how much it will cost to get there, what they will do there and how much money will they need once they arrive. The answer, more often than not, is no, they would never do such a thing. Yet every day, business owners all across the country start businesses without having the answers to these questions: Where are you going? How much will it cost you to get there? What route will you take to get there?

If you wanted to go from California to New York, the first thing you would have to figure out is the mode of transportation. How you should go would be determined by the amount of money you have to spend. If you could not afford to fly, you would have to consider taking a bus or a train or even driving yourself. Also, how much time you would have to get there would enter into your transportation decision.

A business plan is a road map. Just as you take the time to plan a trip—to understand the best route and the costs involved, making allowances for possible detours along the way—so it is when you consider starting your own business. Business planning is mapping the journey–understanding your possible routes, what you are trying to accomplish and your ultimate destination.

Without a business plan, it is very difficult to figure these things out; you end up wandering, drifting, not knowing where you're going. As you begin to think through the planning process, you sort through some of the decisions you need to make. Don't make the mistake of thinking that, because you are developing a microbusiness, fate is enough to take you where you want to go. You must plan. As the saying goes, "To a man who doesn't know where he is going, any road will do." Map your route so you will know the best road to take.

The Importance of Business Planning ━━━━

Since the Small Business Administration began 40 years ago, the failure rate for small businesses has hovered around 90 percent, given a five-year period of operation. It is appalling to me that the rate has stayed so high for so long without efforts to reverse it. I believe that following the plan outlined in this book and understanding all the various components of running a business will empower you to a higher-than-normal level of success.

My clients have had a success rate of 40 percent to 60 percent, compared with the national 10 percent success rate. The reason, quite simply, is that they follow the information and guidance provided in this book.

...writing your own business plan is not about the destination; it's about the journey itself.

I urge each of my clients to create their own business plan. When businesses need capital, often an outsider will write the business plan to be presented to bankers and investors. Unfortunately, having someone else write your business plan does not help you. That's because writing your own business plan is not about the destination; it's about the journey itself. It is about forcing yourself to think through each and every step of making your business happen.

Do not allow the thought of writing a business plan to intimidate you! Many people feel overwhelmed at the thought of writing a business plan. They feel ill prepared to organize such a plan or to predict what might happen to their business in the future. You can take control of the process by breaking the plan into manageable segments. Focus on one segment at a time, work through the information and make the necessary decisions, and then move on to the next segment.

However, if you absolutely cannot write your own plan, don't beat yourself up about it. What's most important is to think it through to develop action steps that will lead you to success. Review the outline of the plan found in the appendix and mentally map out your plan. Although I don't encourage it, it is not unusual for business owners to be in business a year before an actual plan is written.

When writing the plan, be as specific as possible. For example, it's not enough to write that you will use three different marketing strategies at any given time. What are those strategies? What do they cost you? How will you begin to implement them? While writing a business plan, word by word, you begin to better understand how, why, when and what—and the pieces begin to fit together for you. You bond with the plan and then with your business. Once this happens, you will be able to carry it through and be prepared for the detours and obstacles bound to pop up.

Software programs exist for business plans. While I do not recommend them in general, if using one makes it easier for you to get into the mode of developing a business plan, by all means, take advantage of it. The reason I don't recommend these programs is that they are often not thorough enough, and they do so much of the work for you that you end up just dropping in specific details without having to really think through the process. Additionally, they can be confusing, meaning that you don't get the full benefit of using them.

Remember: A business plan is for you. The business plan is not to be written just to turn over to a banker or an investor. The business plan is a tool that will help you be more effective in running a successful business. For it to be useful to you, review it on a regular basis once it is written, making adjustments as necessary. A business plan is always a work in progress. It is never finished, though you may distribute it widely.

When writing a business plan, always write in the third person. Use "it" or "the company" or simply your company's name. That helps you be more objective, focusing on the business, not on you. Don't use "I", "me" or "my".

Strategic Planning

Strategic planning is a more comprehensive form of business planning. It goes beyond the basic business plan, encompassing operational system design and management strategies. The strategic plan is for internal use; should you seek capital and need to submit a business plan, you can extract it from the strategic plan by eliminating the following sections:

- **Management objectives**
- **Organizational structure**
- **Operational systems**
- **Operational controls**
- **Sales strategies**
- **SWOT information**
- **Fee/price structure**

Completing a strategic plan is valuable since it is very comprehensive and forces you to explore every aspect of your business operation. If you are serious about business success, you won't want to do the plan any other way. If you have key workers or associates, involve them in the planning process to allow them to feel more "vested" in the business.

The following discussion details strategic planning, guiding you through the process of developing the comprehensive body of work needed to be in control of your business.

Executive Summary

While the executive summary appears first, it is always written last—after you've completed the plan. The executive summary is a snapshot of the plan itself. It should give possible investors enough information to determine whether they want to read the entire document.

Include the following in the executive summary: an overview of the business, overall goals of the business, its mission and a general strategy for growth. If the business is seeking investors, add the following: how much money is being sought, the interest rate you are hoping to secure, how you will pay it back, the return on the investment and the break-even point for the business. We will discuss return on investment and break-even point later in the chapter. The executive summary should be no more than two pages; one page is even better.

The Company

Under this heading, discuss the business you are in, the category it fits into (graphic art, consulting, manufacturing, retail, etc.), the industry it fits into and your purpose for having this business. Include your purpose statement and mission statement, too. Also discuss here the legal structure of the business: sole proprietorship, partnership, corporation, limited liability company.

PURPOSE STATEMENT. Your purpose statement (speaking strictly about the business) answers four questions: 1) Who are you? 2) What do you do? 3) For whom do you do it? and 4) What benefit do they derive from it?

EXAMPLE: *The Women's Business Training Center is a nonprofit corporation providing business development services to small business owners, helping them to be efficient and profitable.*

This statement should be no more than two sentences that roll easily off your tongue. Use it regularly in public and at networking sessions.

MISSION STATEMENT. The mission statement is a broad statement that has no boundaries, is not quantifiable and has no set time limit. It is a statement of something you want to achieve in operating your business—a goal you are reaching for and working at constantly.

EXAMPLE: *The mission of the Women's Business Training Center is to create economic independence, especially in women, through successful business development.*

Developing your purpose statement and mission statement helps you clarify and easily articulate what you are trying to accomplish with the business.

Company History

Discuss when the business started, using a date such as 1992 or October 1992, instead of stating the number of years since its founding. (Why? Because you never know in what year someone will read your business plan.) Next, discuss why the business began. Perhaps you started the business for one reason, but it has evolved into something different. Discuss your present focus.

Feasibility

In this section, discuss the findings under all the different aspects of feasibility. What has caused you to make the decision to pursue this business? How did you decide who will buy what you sell and at what price? If retail, how did you determine where to locate the shop? If surveys or questionnaires were completed, list the results and discuss the demographics of those involved in the study.

In narrative form, discuss in general the feasibility of the business and demand for what you sell. Cite all evidence uncovered in the research process.

Goals

State short-term and long-term goals (short-term being within two years, long-term beyond that). Without going into the strategies at this time, indicate the goals and the objectives of each. If your goal is to earn $100,000 within the first year of operation, your objectives might include to generate $2,000 a week in revenue through clients or customers. Discuss the steps. The important thing is to think through the managing and measuring of each SMART goal.

Management Team

Even if you are the only person managing the operation, this is your opportunity to outline all of the tasks you perform, such as marketing, administration, sales, record keeping and financial responsibilities. Also discuss the qualifications, experience and separation of responsibilities of the owner and other members of the management team, if any.

Personal Objectives of Management

Outline the motivation of the management team for doing the work of the business. Discuss the separate agendas of the management team with regard to personal goals and how they might conflict or align with the goals of the organization.

This is the section for you to detail your personal goals. Balance out the time, energy and effort you put into the business with personal time. For example, if you have a goal of starting a family, you will want to allow yourself the freedom to do that, yet still understand the impact that it will have on the business. By outlining this in advance, you will be more productive on a personal and professional level.

Whatever your goals are—taking a vacation, buying property, starting a second business—think them through, using the SMART goal-setting model. Think about how those personal goals impact the business goals and what is needed to fulfill both sets of goals.

EXAMPLE: *If you plan to work 10 years and then retire to Tahiti to lie on the beach sipping piña coladas, you will need to work that into your business plan. You'll have to answer questions about how to generate enough revenue to support you and support hiring a capable manager to take over the business. You may have to hire that person well in advance of your 10 year retirement goal.*

It is imperative that you detail the objectives of all the members of your management team to see how their personal goals align with the goals of the organization and your own personal goals. Only then will you understand the strategies needed to make sure that you meet your goals, your employees' goals and the company's goals.

Organizational Structure

This is the section to discuss employees and your company's anticipated growth. How many employees do you anticipate having in the next year, two years, three years and long term? How do you see the business growing over the next 10 years?

It is beneficial here to develop an organizational chart and project, for at least three to five years, what your organization will look like in terms of employees, contractors, subcontractors, and part-time employees. List titles/positions and map out the rules for whomever you expect to be a part of your organization. This will give you a perspective on what needs to be done and when for the organization to progress.

Succession

Too often, business owners neglect to plan for the time they can no longer function in their business. If you were to die or become disabled, how would your business continue? A sole proprietorship, for example, by law is automatically dissolved upon the death of the owner. If you are interested in preserving your business, provide in writing for someone else to take it over. Answer these questions now, not just before your anticipated retirement time.

It's a good idea to plan to train someone to take over and to outline this in your will. Regardless of whether you feel you have enough assets to write a will, having one will prove beneficial down the road.

SWOT: Strengths, Weaknesses, Opportunities and Threats

Carefully review the traits you listed under each of the elements of the SWOT exercise in Chapter Six. In this section, list the traits, as well as the strategies you intend to use to improve on the strengths and weaknesses. Discuss how you will use the skills and knowledge of others to supplement your weaknesses and balance your strengths. Speak to the opportunities and threats you see for yourself and your business. How will you deal with them?

Industry Data and Competition

Here is the place to detail the information, previously discussed, that you have gathered about your industry. Discuss the six points of your industry as detailed in Chapter Eight. They are:

1. **Size and nature of the industry,**
2. **Competition,**
3. **Growth prospects,**
4. **Structure: suppliers, cost, distribution,**
5. **Trends and development,**
6. **Impact of technology.**

Market Information

Include here the results of your market research: your target market, your niche, demographic information, market surveys, etc. Once you have identified who is likely to purchase your product or service, detail your marketing strategies to reach them.

Product/Service

This section allows you to detail what makes your product, service or approach different from the competition. What philosophies/concepts make you different?

_____

EXAMPLE: *My own business uses a holistic approach that deals with the whole person, not just the business. We make sure that the person gets the necessary support, encouragement and time to build confidence levels and to overcome fears. That is a very different approach than that of most business consultants, spend most of their time dealing specifically with business issues. I believe a business cannot succeed without making sure the business owner feels empowered to make capable and effective business decisions.*

_____

There are only three things that you can do in marketing to make an impression: You can be the best, you can be No. 1 or you can be different. While it is very difficult to be No. 1 or the best in doing anything, it is not so difficult to be different. If you choose to be different, finding that niche and providing goods or services that are different will require a certain strategy. Look for opportunities that allow you to be different. It will work to your advantage.

In this section, discuss how you run your business and why. How do your business methods serve your clients, and are you successful? Discuss how you plan to measure your performance—evaluations and questionnaires are examples. Discuss the economic benefits to your customers. Ask yourself what methods you plan to use to provide a certain quality of service and/or products. Are you planning any improvements? How will customers receive your information or products?

Price/Fee Structure

Once you have done your cost analysis, discuss the pricing structure you will use, the reasons for using it and how you will go about making adjustments to prices/fees set.

Credit Policy

In this portion of your business plan, outline your credit policy (if you have one), with all of the conditions for credit, e.g., return policy, late fee and interest rate, if any.

Sales Strategies

This is the place to outline step-by-step the strategies you choose to accomplish your goals. Discuss how you will break your goals into manageable segments and what action you will take to achieve your objectives. How do you plan to measure the progress of your goals?

Also in this section, discuss any in-house sales support. For example, if a person has a problem beyond the scope of customer service, do you plan any kind of technical support to help him or her better understand product instructions? Ask yourself if there are presale costs and whether you have to buy raw materials before selling something. Will you need to spend money to develop a proposal before any service/product is actually sold?

Manufacturing Considerations

If you will manufacture a product, begin by discussing the kind and amount of equipment you have, the layout and the tooling. Layout is critical in terms of being efficient and cost-effective. Minimize movement in completing a task and you minimize your costs.

List production information, such as any manufacturing limitations. For example, you would discuss the fact that your equipment is not as modern as others on the market, lessening your output. Outline any plans to improve your equipment over time.

Discuss in detail your work scheduling. Are there second and third shifts? Who handles packaging and how? Discuss who will be responsible for shipping and handling and whether it will be done in-house or by an outside contractor.

Also detail how you plan to handle inspection systems and quality control. How will you make sure production is done right? How will you factor in mistakes?

If you contract out your production, how will you make sure the job gets done without wasted materials, time and money? By all rights, you should have a quality-control person in the plant of the contractor, as long as you produce on a regular basis. This person monitors your production to make sure that you maximize efficiency at all times.

By the same token, if you manufacture your own product, quality control should be one of your greatest concerns. It is one of the easiest ways to keep costs down. It is usually worthwhile to hire a good quality-control person to ensure maximum efficiency and cost effectiveness.

...how will you make sure the job gets done without wasted materials, time and money?

Also detail inventory requirements in this section–how much inventory you need to maintain at any given time. Keeping inventory and maintaining inventory records is as simple or as complex as the particular system you put in place.

Retail Operation

If yours is a retail business, discuss purchasing and inventory budgets here, including how you handle inventory control. Is it done through a computerized cash register, another computerized system or manually? What is your "open to buy" policy? Will purchases be based on a set annual budget or on sales? Describe the system here, as well as any other purchasing strategies.

Also discuss your strategy for handling theft and pilferage: security system, alarms, monitors, cameras, etc. Include a discussion of the store itself, such as existing and new fixtures. Detail how your space will change once your business grows, as well as your plans for products that do not sell within a certain time.

Operational System Design

In this section discuss the different internal systems you will use to handle day-to-day situations in the business. What kinds of forms will you generate? How will your informational and record keeping systems function? What policies and procedures will you put in place?

Operational Controls

Controlling how work gets done is vital. Ask yourself what kind of controls you will implement to make sure employees complete work in a timely way. (Include yourself in this discussion.) Will you have summary reports to indicate work completed on a weekly and/or monthly basis? Will you discuss and evaluate the results of goals on a regular basis? How will you institute these controls?

Pro Forma

This is the financial section, in which you project income and expenses, cash flow and other financial indicators. If you have been in business for a while, you'll need to include the financial history of the business, including startup costs and when you broke even. Include plans for expansion in a budget separate from the operating budget.

FINANCIAL PROJECTIONS. There are plenty of spreadsheet computer programs for doing financial projections. If you do not have a computer, I encourage you to get one, as it will increase your efficiency tenfold. Format your computer spreadsheet so that you have 14 columns. The left column is for line items, then a column for each of the 12 months and a column on the far right for totals. You can also do projections manually with 13-column accounting paper. An accountant can help you devise the system that works best for you and can help you understand how to do it on your own. (See Chapter Thirteen for examples of spreadsheets and financial projections.)

Financial projections need to be done at least three years into the future. The first year will be month-by-month, with the second and third years done quarterly. In projecting income, I recommend that you decide how much you want to earn monthly. You can arrive at this figure in several different ways. One is to estimate your monthly earnings based on the amount of work you expect to get for the money you spend each month on marketing. Or, you can set a goal of annual earnings, take it through the SMART goal-setting model to make sure it is within your grasp and capacity, then divide it into monthly segments to understand how realistic your goals are.

It's important, when projecting, to realize that not all months will be the same. It usually takes time to have a decent amount of money flowing in, unless your products or services are so much in demand that people are banging at your door.

Expect to start off slow. Always project low for income and high for expenses. Be realistic; put your goals in proper perspective. For your own benefit, break down the different ways you plan to derive your income from the business.

EXAMPLE: *as a consultant, you may generate income from direct contact with clients, speaking engagements, training sessions you conduct and from your products, such as books and tapes.*

Although there are fixed and variable expenses, it is not necessary to break them down into those categories. Instead, your accountant can discuss with you GAAP (Generally Acceptable Accounting Principles) required by the government and used as a business standard for all accounting reports.

Projecting is not difficult if you take the time to think through the process. Correlate your financial projections to the goals you have set, especially those goals that relate to how much money you expect to earn over the next three years.

CASH FLOW ANALYSIS. Once you have completed your financial projections, you need to do a cash flow analysis. This is simply plotting out income and expenses according to when it is realistic to expect that they will actually occur.

Always project low for income and high for expenses.

EXAMPLE: *You earn money in January, yet because of your client's payment system, you know that you will not receive any income from this project for two months. So while you earned it in January, you will plot it on the cash flow analysis in March because that's when the money actually comes in.*

By the same token, if you receive a phone bill in January, you often do not have to pay it until February, so plot your payment in February. If you plot income and expenses into the correct months, you will gain a sense of how your money will flow. Cash flow analysis is critical to help you anticipate any shortfalls.

Many businesses make enough money during the year to cover all expenses, with money left over. However, during the course of that year there may be lean periods in which cash is not available, making it necessary to either have a cash reserve or to borrow funds. This is why completing the cash flow analysis is important.

Projecting a year in advance enables you to anticipate shortfalls. This gives you time to plan—perhaps by talking to a bank in advance. All too often, companies are edged out of business just by not understanding cash flow and not being prepared for the shortfalls bound to happen. And it's much easier to finance your expected shortfall if you can show, through your cash flow analysis, that the business will generate enough income to cover expenses and support the debt. Finance will be discussed in more depth in the following chapter. (See Chapter Thirteen for examples of cash flow analyses.)

RETURN ON INVESTMENT. Return on investment is another formula of interest to small business owners. It helps you to understand how much of the money you put into your business you can expect to have returned in a particular year. The formula for return on investment is "Net Income after Tax divided by Investment." Investors usually will not consider investing in your business without at least a 20 percent return on investment during your first year of business.

Conclusion

Strategic planning and all that is included in building a sound plan will provide you with valuable information from which to base business decisions. Planning is without question the single most important task you can perform, whether for startups or for maintaining control of a business on an ongoing basis. Plan well and you will reap the benefits of increased profits and peace of mind. Remember, when you fail to plan, you are actually planning to fail!

CHAPTER TWELVE

The ABCs of Business Finance

What is Accounting, and Why is it Important?

If you are like most small business owners, the whole idea of record keeping and taking care of the financial aspects of your business is a bit overwhelming. It need not be. By following some simple guidelines, accounting can actually become a tool for you to understand how best to move your business forward. If you overcome the fear of accounting and look at it as a means to collect and analyze data, you will soon look forward to the record keeping process. It will help you to make intelligent, informed decisions about your business.

Accounting is not just bookkeeping and the recording of your income and expenses. It is also an analysis, a review and comparison of records to produce periodic statements that assess the status of the business and measure progress. Without doing the accounting, you do not have a basis to assess where you are nor to measure the progress you have made towards your goal or towards building a successful business.

Record Keeping.

What is record keeping? It is primarily the detailing of income and expenses as well as various other aspects of running a business. Any records about the business–client lists, shipping and receiving documents, sales records, time sheets, payroll records and fixed assets–are part of your record keeping system.

SAFE SPEED LIMIT 55

Not all of them relate to the financial aspects. It could be client information so you can analyze and extract client data. That is still a form of record keeping. A good record keeping system is:

- **Simple to use,**
- **Easy to understand,**
- **Reliable,**
- **Accurate,**
- **Consistent,**
- **Designed to provide information on a timely basis.**

What exactly does that last point mean? To maintain effective records, make sure to keep information in a systematic way and to record it on a regular basis so that you can access the information at any given time for any reason. Also make sure you have a clear picture of when the information was collected and what it applies to, and clearly state various time considerations.

Journals and Ledgers

You will need several tools to keep financial records. The first is called a journal, which is nothing more than a written record of business transactions. Information for the journal comes from original source documents, such as sales slips, check stubs, checkbook register, receipts and purchase orders. Anything that is the original source for information can be used to enter information into a journal. Documentation is needed for every transaction to establish a "paper trail" for your business to justify monies and items coming into or going out of your business.

Typically, a journal entry will show debits and credits in the order in which they occur. Double-entry bookkeeping dictates that if one account is debited, then another account must be credited in order to maintain balance.

Another tool you will need is the ledger, which details income and expenses by categories. When accountants set up ledgers, they use numbers to identify individual accounts or categories. This is usually called the Chart of Accounts. When information from the journal is entered onto the ledger, it is called "posting." Items regularly posted to the ledger give you information to analyze and document what is going on in your business. The ledger also generates financial reports, preferably on a regular basis.

For tax purposes, you need to save all of your receipts to document your journal entries and maintain the "paper trail." A convenient way to do this is to carry an envelope in your daily appointment book for your day-to-day expenses such as gas and parking receipts. Keep a separate envelope for each month. Maintain another monthly envelope or folder in the office to keep all your receipts.

Number and keep any receipts that you write so that you may enter the information into whatever kind of accounting system you are using. Failure to carefully record receipts can cause problems for you when filing your taxes.

It is important for you to have the whole financial picture of your company. Business records are like unexposed rolls of film. You must develop them before you can see all of the pictures. Facts and figures must be arranged in an orderly manner for you to have that clear picture of your business.

Accountants vs. Bookkeepers

To analyze that picture, you should have a competent accountant review your accounting reports to interpret your business situation. The best computer or manual accounting systems will not work if you are not experienced in maintaining proper accounting records. If that is the case, find someone who can instruct you initially on how to set up your systems and how to maintain them effectively so that you collect pertinent and necessary information to meet the requirements of city, state and federal governments.

An accountant is often a Certified Public Accountant (CPA), regulated by state guidelines requiring certain standards of knowledge. Whether certified or not, an accountant should have a high level of expertise in whatever area of accounting he or she practices. In selecting an accountant, find someone well versed in the area of small and micro businesses, because your accounting situation will be very different from a large corporation, and tax implications are extremely different. Ask around, check references of other microbusinesses an accountant has served. The most valuable areas for which to seek accounting consultation are:

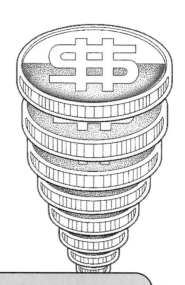

- **Setting up the accounting system and advice on which system is best,**

- **Filing taxes on a quarterly or annual basis,**

- **Any major change in operations: expansion, dissolution, need for a loan or line of credit.**

An accountant costs more per hour than a bookkeeper, sometimes twice as much or more, so often the decision of whether to hire a bookkeeper or an accountant is based on finances.

A bookkeeper is trained in maintaining business records and uses Generally Accepted Accounting Principles (GAAP), just as accountants. (GAAP, instituted several decades ago for record keeping by the Internal Revenue Service, mandates that all business accounting adhere to certain formats and guidelines to facilitate a uniform method of keeping records that is easily interpreted for tax purposes.) A bookkeeper usually does not have the same education level of an accountant; however, a skilled bookkeeper is usually as effective as an accountant in a particular area of accounting. A bookkeeper usually can maintain journals, post information to the ledger, generate financial reports, maintain payroll information and write checks for your signature. It is expedient to have a bookkeeper and an accountant for tax preparation.

Often, small business owners cannot afford to have a bookkeeper on staff. If you do the necessary recording, save expense receipts and issue receipts when you collect money, a part-time or free-lance bookkeeper can input that information into your accounting system once a month so that you will always have well-maintained records. Once you are shown how to do this, it should be easy to maintain.

Filing taxes is a different matter. Whether you must file quarterly or annually, use an experienced accountant to prepare the proper tax forms. If you have used a bookkeeper or maintained the records properly yourself, the accountant will have the proper information and it will cost you less than if the accountant has to sort out all of the information before completing the tax forms.

Another cost-efficient alternative is to have a business consultant review your system. Your local Small Business Development Center 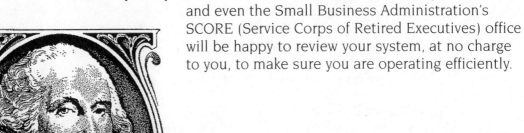 and even the Small Business Administration's SCORE (Service Corps of Retired Executives) office will be happy to review your system, at no charge to you, to make sure you are operating efficiently.

What You Should Know About Your Business Accounting

So, what are those records that you need to maintain? You should know, on a *daily basis*:

- **Your cash on hand,**

- **Your bank balance for personal and business accounts (keep separate at all times),**

- **The daily sales summary,**

- **Cash receipts,**

- **Monies paid out.**

Any errors that come up in recording collections on accounts should be noted and brought to your attention. All of these five things are very important to you, as the business owner. If you a product of any kind, know how many were produced on any given day, and maintain records for each day.

Too often, business owners write checks without having balanced their books on an on-going basis and with no awareness of how much money is in the account. If you write checks on funds that are not available, your bank record will suffer. Banking relationships are very critical in obtaining any loan or line of credit you might need as your business begins to grow.

On a *weekly basis*, you should know:

- **Accounts receivable (how much money is owed to you),**

- **Accounts payable (how much money you owe),**

- **Payroll data (how much you owe for payroll this week),**

- **What taxes you owe.**

Reports should be made to state and federal governments as required by law. In regard to payroll information, at the time payroll is done, you should be aware of what the payroll taxes are associated with that particular payroll. Often, business owners will only pay taxes once a month, but if you are meeting payroll weekly, you need to know on a weekly basis what the taxes are to be sure that funds will be available to meet your payroll responsibilities every month.

Often business owners write payroll checks only once or twice a month so that funds can remain in the account as long as possible. Hopefully it is an interest-bearing account so that interest can accumulate to your benefit rather than to the bank's benefit. Take a look at how you handle your payroll situation. Consider issuing payroll checks once a month or every two weeks, not on a weekly basis, which ultimately costs you more money.

On a *monthly basis*, you should:

- **Post journal entries to a general ledger.**

- **Develop a report showing profit or loss to the business.**

- **Generate a balance sheet.**

- **Reconcile bank statements to make sure everything balances out.**

- **Balance petty cash account.**

- **Deposit all federal taxes in the bank, as required by law (only if you have employees).**

- **Pay state taxes as agreed. If the state has informed you that you must make state payroll taxes on a monthly basis, then you need to know what they are and make sure to allocate funds.**

- **Age past due accounts receivables. In other words, it is important to you to know what money is owed and how long it has been owed.**

- **Know your inventory.**

Proactive Record Keeping

Accounts receivable aging is very important to businesses that allow credit. Often, the fact that someone has not paid you monthly as agreed slips past you. If you do not pay attention, the bill could become three or four months behind. A past due account is money out of your pocket and begins to hurt you in terms of your overall accounting for the business. Cash flow is money coming into and money going out of the business. Your ability to project your cash flow is directly impacted by the way you handle your receivables. Negative cash flows can cause you to be out of business before you realize what hit you.

Bankers tell me that negative cash flow due to failure to collect funds owed is a major factor in business failures. If banks are to consider loaning you money, they will want to know how you manage your finances. If you have accounts that are three, four or five months past due, banks will not look favorably upon that.

Staying in control of your receivables allows you to be proactive about your record keeping. Make sure that you are taking the necessary action on slow payers. Set up a system whereby if an account is 30 days late, you send a letter. If an account is 45 days late, maybe a second letter should go out. An account that is 60 days late may require a phone call. A common mistake that microbusiness owners make is to "finance" their customers and clients at no charge by not collecting their receivables. Bankers are quick to observe this when reviewing a business's financial records.

Develop and maintain a system that keeps you aware of accounts as they age. Determine the appropriate action and take it. This allows you to stay on top of the money owed to you. If clients or customer owe money more than 60 days past due, you may need to cut off the supply or no longer provide them with service. Make the decision as to when the cut-off point should be and remain in control of what is going on.

Also be aware of inventory on a monthly basis. If you make products or sell items, you should maintain and review the stock condition monthly so that you know at all times where you stand and what your re-order situation is. You may need to re-order more product or raw materials. If you do not stay on top of it and do not have a system for just that, it will be very difficult to know when you need to order additional raw materials.

Another way to be proactive is to take advantage of all discounts on payables. If you owe money and are offered a discount to pay on time or within a short period of time, try to arrange your finances such that you can take advantage of those discounts. They add up over time. Make sure you maintain detailed records from which you can determine, at any given point, where you stand financially in running your business. Pay taxes as they are due. If you do not, you may not have a business to operate for very long. The Internal Revenue Service, as well as most state government agencies, are very strict about enforcing taxes that are due and payable.

If you have employees, you will be responsible for deducting federal taxes from the earnings of each and paying additional federal taxes based on a percentage of what is deducted for the employees. These taxes will be due monthly depending on the total amount of your payroll.

If you owe state income taxes, know when those taxes are due, and pay them. If you fall behind on paying either your state or federal taxes, either entity can seize your records and business, put a lock on your door and cause you to cease operations. It doesn't take a lot for that to happen, so stay abreast of what is going on and make sure to pay taxes on a regular basis.

Are you wasting a lot of time by not being organized and not being able to find things?

Generate financial reports regularly so that you can see where you are in operating your business. If you are a very small operation, completing financial reports quarterly may be enough for you to truly have a sense of where you are, how much money you are pulling in and how much money you are paying out. Doing so can help you determine what actions you might need to take to generate more revenues or to cut expenses so that you can have greater profits. If you are not generating reports, there is no way for you to see the financial situation of the business, or to truly understand the strategies needed to overcome problems or to even be able to identify problems. Without reports, you cannot move forward with any confidence.

Take appropriate action to eliminate waste and losses. If you have employees, or even if you work alone, step back and take a look at how you do business. What could you do differently? Are you wasting a lot of time by not being organized and not being able to find things? Are you duplicating your efforts by doing things over because you do not remember where you filed it or what happened to it or whether it was done at all? Stay in control of your operation and take the appropriate steps to eliminate waste at all costs.

Choosing A Record Keeping System

So, what record keeping system should you choose? What accounting program is the best for your particular operation? The answer depends on how much money you have to spend on the system, your familiarity with accounting, and what kind of support and programs you might need to help you. More importantly, it depends on whether you have a computer. If you have no computer and no plans to get one any time soon, there are several manual systems that might be of benefit to you. Even though they are fairly "antiquated," manual bookkeeping systems are still an effective way to maintain information for the business.

The Dome Bookkeeping System is one that has been in effect for many years and still provides quality information, even though it requires you to manually list journal and ledger entries. This system offers weekly or monthly systems. These systems list details of your expenditures, show detailed category listings for all of those expenditures and offer progressive totals: monthly, to-this-month and to-this-date. It is a good system that provides an effective way to monitor your business finances.

Another manual system is called the "one-write" system. One-write systems are produced by a number of different manufacturers. Each provides you with a simplified way to write a check and make a journal entry at the same time. Imprinted, duplicate checks are attached to journal sheets, and, as checks are written, the journal entry occurs. The carbonless copies of each check written can serve as a voucher or be maintained for your records. There is a bank balance column, a deposit column with room for a description, and 42 columns for categorizing expenses of your choice. Double-window envelopes elim-inate the need to address the envelope, as the check has space for the payee's address.

The "one-write" system is a very handy way to maintain good records and not worry about posting a check to the journal because the register doubles as a journal. The system is fairly inexpensive. Safeguard is one manufacturer that produces it. Deluxe has a system, as well. It probably costs less than $100 to get started with this kind of set up, including checks, envelopes and the journal binder.

If you have a computer, computerized systems do not cost more than $150 to $200 to set up, in addition to your checks. They provide you with a tremendous amount of tools over manual systems. Computerized systems simplify your financial record keeping. There are a number of computerized accounting sys-tems available on the market today. Pay attention to whether the system does double-entry bookkeeping. A double-entry sys-tem has more checks and balances and will provide you with a better accounting system than a single-entry system.

EXAMPLE: *Quicken is a single-entry system. Though it is easy to use and generates a number of different reports, it does not provide all the tools and benefits necessary to get a wide variety of accurate reports with which to run your business. Peachtree and QuickBooks are two that do. While there are many others on the market that also provide double-entry systems, Peachtree and QuickBooks are probably the oldest and have most of the bugs worked out of them. While I am not trying to make a recommendation to you, Peachtree does provide better, more understandable reports than QuickBooks.*

Some of the reports these systems provide are profit and loss statements, income statements and balance sheets. You can generate many other reports that will assist you in making solid business decisions based on information rather than gut feeling or emotion or what you think might be going on in your business. As long as the information entered into the computer system is accurate, the reports generated will be accurate.

These reports can be a valuable tool for making business decisions. You can also develop graphs and charts from the information entered. If you are not currently using a computerized system and you have a business that is up and running, or if you anticipate getting your business off the ground in the near future, take the time to explore computerized systems, especially if you have a computer or are planning to buy one.

CHAPTER THIRTEEN

Financial Forecasting and Reporting

Financial Definitions

The following definitions will help you better understand how to develop projections and reports in keeping with GAAP and prepare you to focus on the exhibits used in this chapter:

Current assets. Those easily liquidated within 12 months.

Fixed assets. Those having a life of more than one year and used to produce or distribute goods and services.

Accounts receivable. Funds owed the business on goods or services delivered.

Accounts payable. Monies owed by the business.

Current liabilities. Debts that are due within one year.

Long-term liabilities. Those not fully payable within the next 12 months.

Inventory. Goods to be sold or raw materials to be manufactured.

Depreciation. A deduction method to recover cost of property over its useful life.

Notes payable. Usually loans with interest and monthly payments.

Owner's equity. Value of the owner's interest in the business after liabilities are deducted from assets.

Draw. monies distributed to the owner in the current year.

Retained earnings. Current year's profit per the income statement.

Sales. Source of income.

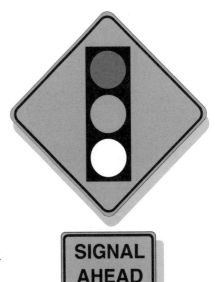

Exhibit A1

BROWDER OFFICE SUPPORT SERVICES
INCOME AND EXPENSES PROJECTIONS
JULY 1996 - JUNE 1997

INCOME	July	Aug	Sept	Oct	Nov	Dec	Jan	Feb	Mar	Apr	May	Jun	TOTALS
Sales	18,000	17,000	17,000	16,000	16,000	17,000	18,000	17,000	17,000	16,000	18,000	18,000	205,000
Total Income	**18,000**	**17,000**	**17,000**	**16,000**	**16,000**	**17,000**	**18,000**	**17,000**	**17,000**	**16,000**	**18,000**	**18,000**	**205,000**
EXPENSES													
Salaries/wages	6,345	6,345	6,345	6,345	6,345	6345	6345	6,345	6,345	6,345	6,345	6,345	76,140
Payroll tax/fringe	1,396	1,396	1,396	1,396	1,396	1,396	1,396	1,396	1,396	1,396	1,396	1,396	16,752
Rent	650	650	650	650	650	650	650	650	650	650	650	650	7800
Utilities	45	45	30	30	35	35	35	35	35	35	35	35	430
Phone/fax/cellular	225	225	225	225	225	225	225	225	225	225	225	225	2700
Ofc expenses/ printing	25	25	25	25	25	25	25	25	25	25	25	25	300
Postage & delivery	80	80	80	80	80	80	80	80	80	80	80	80	960
Equipment	250	250	250	250	250	250	250	250	250	250	250	250	3000
Depreciation	200	200	200	200	200	200	200	200	200	200	200	200	2400
Travel/entertainment	100	100	100	100	100	100	100	100	100	100	100	100	1200
Auto expense	300	300	300	300	300	300	300	300	300	300	300	300	3600
Insurance	320	320	320	320	320	320	320	320	320	320	320	320	3840
Marketing	280	280	280	280	280	280	280	280	280	280	280	280	3360
Legal services	200	0	200	0	200	0	0	200	0	0	400	200	1400
Accounting services	200	0	0	400	0	200	0	0	400	0	200	0	1400
Contributions	0	0	0	0	0	0	0	0	200	200	200	200	800
Miscellaneous	200	200	200	200	200	200	200	200	200	200	200	200	2400
Owner's draw	3,000	3,000	3,000	3,000	3,000	3,000	3,000	3,000	3,000	3,000	3,000	3,000	36,000
Total Expenses	13,816	13,416	13,601	13,801	13,606	13,606	13,406	13,606	14,006	13,606	14,206	13,806	164,482
Total Income	**18,000**	**17,000**	**17,000**	**16,000**	**16,000**	**17,000**	**18,000**	**17,000**	**17,000**	**16,000**	**18,000**	**18,000**	**205,000**
Net Income	4,184	3,584	3,399	2,199	2,394	3,394	4,594	3,394	2,994	2,394	3,794	4,194	40,518
Fed. Income Tax	1,108	1,108	1,108	1,109	1,108	1,108	1,109	1,108	1,108	1,109	1,108	1,109	13,300
Net Profit	3,076	2,476	2,291	1,090	1,286	2,286	3,485	2,286	1,886	1,285	2,686	3,085	27,218

Exhibit A2

BROWDER OFFICE SUPPORT SERVICES
CASH FLOW PROJECTIONS
JULY 1996 - JUNE 1997

	July	Aug	Sept	Oct	Nov	Dec	Jan	Feb	Mar	Apr	May	Jun	TOTALS
INCOME													
Sales	16,000	18,000	13,000	17,000	15,000	15,000	17,000	15,000	17,000	15,000	16,000	18,000	192,000
Total Income	**16,000**	**18,000**	**13,000**	**17,000**	**15,000**	**15,000**	**17,000**	**15,000**	**17,000**	**15,000**	**16,000**	**18,000**	**192,000**
EXPENSES													
Salaries/wages	6,345	6,345	6,345	6,345	6,345	6345	6345	6,345	6,345	6,345	6,345	6,345	76,140
Payroll tax/fringe	1,396	1,396	1,396	1,396	1,396	1,396	1,396	1,396	1,396	1,396	1,396	1,396	16,752
Rent	650	650	650	650	650	650	650	650	650	650	650	650	7800
Utilities	45	30	30	35	35	35	35	35	35	35	35	35	420
Phone/fax/cellular	225	225	225	225	225	225	225	225	225	225	225	225	2700
Ofc expenses/ printing	25	25	25	25	25	25	25	25	25	25	25	25	300
Postage & delivery	80	80	80	80	80	80	80	80	80	80	80	80	960
Equipment	250	250	250	250	250	250	250	250	250	250	250	250	3000
Travel/entertainment	100	100	100	100	100	100	100	100	100	100	100	100	1200
Auto expense	300	300	300	300	300	300	300	300	300	300	300	300	3600
Insurance	320	320	320	320	320	320	320	320	320	320	320	320	3840
Marketing	280	280	280	280	280	280	280	280	280	280	280	280	3360
Legal services	200	0	200	0	200	0	0	200	0	0	400	200	1400
Accounting services	200	0	0	400	0	200	0	0	400	0	200	0	1400
Contributions	0	0	0	0	0	0	0	0	0	0	0	0	800
Miscellaneous	200	200	200	200	200	200	200	200	200	200	200	200	2400
Owner's draw	3,000	3,000	3,000	3,000	3,000	3,000	3,000	3,000	3,000	3,000	3,000	3,000	36,000
Total Expenses	13,616	13,201	13,401	13,606	13,406	13,406	13,206	13,406	13,806	13,406	14,006	13,606	162,072
Net Income	2,384	4,799	-401	3,394	1,594	1,594	3,794	1,594	3,194	1,594	1,994	4,394	29,928
Fed. Income Tax	3,324	0	0	3,325	0	0	3,325	0	0	3,325	0	0	13,299
Beginning Balance	0	-940	3,859	3,458	3,527	5,121	6,715	7,184	8,778	11,972	10,241	12,235	
Total Income	**16,000**	**18,000**	**13,000**	**17,000**	**15,000**	**15,000**	**17,000**	**15,000**	**17,000**	**15,000**	**16,000**	**18,000**	**192,000**
Cash Flow	16,940	13,201	13,401	16,931	13,406	13,406	16,531	13,806	13,806	16,731	14,006	13,606	16,629
Net Cash Flow	-940	3,859	3,458	3,527	5,121	6,715	7,184	8,778	11,972	10,241	12,235	16,629	16,629

Exhibit B1

SUSIE'S SILKS
PROJECTED INCOME AND EXPENSES
JANUARY - DECEMBER 1997

INCOME	Jan	Feb	Mar	Apr	May	Jun	Jul	Aug	Sept	Oct	Nov	Dec	TOTALS
Sales	13,000	12,800	12,900	13,000	13,000	14,000	13,200	13,000	13,500	14,000	13,800	13,700	159,900
Cost of Sales	1,700	2,000	1,670	1,800	1,500	1,400	1,700	1,800	1,700	1,600	1,600	1,700	20,170
Gross Profit	**11,300**	**10,800**	**11,230**	**11,200**	**11,500**	**12,600**	**11,500**	**11,200**	**11,800**	**12,400**	**12,200**	**12,000**	**139,730**
EXPENSES													
Rent	950	950	950	950	950	950	950	950	950	950	950	950	11400
Utilities	45	45	30	30	35	35	35	35	35	35	35	35	430
Phone/fax/cellular	150	150	150	150	150	150	150	150	150	150	150	150	1800
Ofc expenses/ printing	245	50	50	50	100	50	50	50	100	50	50	50	895
Postage & delivery	135	140	150	150	170	170	170	165	165	165	165	165	1910
Equipment/furn	250	450	200	250	200	200	200	200	200	300	300	300	3050
Depreciation	85	85	85	85	85	85	85	85	85	85	85	85	1020
Travel/entertainment	225	225	225	225	225	225	225	225	225	225	225	225	2700
Auto expense	150	150	150	150	150	150	150	150	150	150	150	150	1800
Insurance	125	125	125	125	125	125	125	125	125	125	125	125	1500
Marketing	600	600	600	600	600	600	600	600	600	600	600	600	7200
Legal services	200	0	0	0	0	0	0	400	0	0	0	0	600
Accounting services	0	0	0	400	0	200	0	0	0	0	0	400	1000
Miscellaneous	200	200	200	200	200	200	200	200	200	200	200	200	2400
Owner's draw	4,000	4,000	4,000	4,000	4,000	4,000	4,000	4,000	4,000	4,000	4,000	4,000	48,000
Total Expenses	**7,360**	**7,170**	**6,915**	**7,365**	**6,990**	**7,140**	**6,940**	**7,335**	**6,985**	**7,035**	**7,035**	**7,435**	**85,705**
Gross Profit	**11,300**	**10,800**	**11,230**	**11,200**	**11,500**	**12,600**	**11,500**	**11,200**	**11,800**	**12,400**	**12,200**	**12,000**	**139,730**
Net Income	3,940	3,630	4,315	3,835	4,510	5,460	4,560	3,865	4,815	5,365	5,165	4,565	54,025
Fed. Income Tax	1,391	1,344	1,447	1,376	1,477	1,419	1,484	1,380	1,522	1,608	1,575	1,485	17,508
Net Profit	2,549	2,286	2,868	2,459	3,033	4,041	3,076	2,485	3,293	3,757	3,590	3,080	36,517

Exhibit B2

SUSIE'S SILK
CASH FLOW PROJECTIONS
JANUARY - DECEMBER 1997

	Jan	Feb	Mar	Apr	May	Jun	Jul	Aug	Sept	Oct	Nov	Dec	TOTALS
INCOME													
Sales	9,500	10,000	10,500	11,000	10,000	11,000	9,950	10,000	10,500	14,000	12,000	12,000	130,450
Cost of sales	1,700	2,000	1,670	1,800	1,500	1,400	1,700	1,800	1,700	1,600	1,600	1,700	20,170
Gross Profit	**7,800**	**8,000**	**8,830**	**9,200**	**8,500**	**9,600**	**8,250**	**8,200**	**8,800**	**12,400**	**10,400**	**10,300**	**110,280**
EXPENSES													
Rent	950	950	950	950	950	950	950	950	950	950	950	950	11400
Utilities	45	45	30	30	35	35	35	35	35	35	35	35	430
Phone/fax/cellular	150	150	150	150	150	150	150	150	150	150	150	150	1800
Ofc expenses/ printing	245	50	50	50	100	50	50	50	100	50	50	50	895
Postage & delivery	135	140	150	150	170	170	170	165	165	165	165	165	1910
Equipment/furn	250	450	200	650	0	0	900	0	0	150	150	300	3050
Travel/entertainment	625	25	25	625	25	25	625	25	25	625	25	25	2700
Auto expense	150	150	150	150	150	150	150	150	150	150	150	150	1800
Insurance	0	0	0	1,500	0	0	0	0	0	0	0	0	1500
Marketing	600	600	1,800	600	0	600	0	1,800	600	0	600	0	7200
Legal services	600	0	0	0	0	0	0	0	0	0	0	0	600
Accounting services	0	0	0	0	0	1,000	0	0	0	0	0	0	1000
Miscellaneous	200	200	200	200	200	200	200	200	200	200	200	200	2400
Owner's draw	4,000	4,000	4,000	4,000	4,000	4,000	4,000	4,000	4,000	4,000	4,000	4,000	48,000
Total Expenses	**7,950**	**6,760**	**7,705**	**9,055**	**5,780**	**7,330**	**7,230**	**7,525**	**6,375**	**6,475**	**6,475**	**6,025**	**84,685**
Net Income	-150	1,240	1,125	145	2,720	2,270	1,020	675	2,425	5,925	3,925	4,275	25,595
Fed. Income Tax	0	0	0	4,182	0	0	4,272	0	0	4,386	0	0	12,840
Beginning Balance	0	-150	1,090	2,215	-1,822	898	3,168	-84	591	3,016	4,555	8,480	
Gross Profit	**7,800**	**8,000**	**8,830**	**9,200**	**8,500**	**9,600**	**8,250**	**8,200**	**8,800**	**12,400**	**10,400**	**10,300**	**110,280**
Cash Flow	7,950	6,760	7,705	13,237	5,780	7,330	11,502	7,525	6,375	10,861	6,475	6,025	6,025
Net Cash Flow	-150	1,090	2,215	-1,822	898	3,168	-84	591	3,016	4,555	8,480	12,755	12,755

Exhibit C1

BROWDER OFFICE SUPPORT SERVICES
INCOME STATEMENT
For 8 months ended February 28, 1997

	CURRENT MONTH		YEAR-TO-DATE	
	ACTUAL	PERCENT	ACTUAL	PERCENT
Sales (income)	$18,000	100%	$144,000	100%
Gross Profit	$18,000	100%	144,000	100%
Operating Expenses				
Salaries & wages	9,345	51.9	75,640	52.5
Payroll taxes/fringe	2,055	11.4	16,641	11.6
Professional fees	250	1.4	2,500	1.7
Rent	650	3.6	5,200	3.6
Utilities	35	0.2	320	0.2
Phone/fax/cellular	225	1.2	1,960	1.4
Office supplies	25	0.1	350	0.2
Postage & delivery	103	0.6	915	0.6
Equipment	370	2.1	4,200	2.9
Depreciation	230	1.3	1,900	1.3
Travel/entertainment	74	0.4	678	0.5
Auto expense	286	1.6	2,288	1.6
Insurance	320	1.8	2,560	1.8
Marketing	235	1.3	2,200	1.5
Contributions	0	0	200	0.1
Miscellaneous	118	0.7	1,020	0.7
Total Expenses	14,321	79.6	118,572	82.3
Net Income	3,679	20.4 %	25,428	17.7 %

Exhibit C2

BROWDER OFFICE SUPPORT SERVICES
BUDGETED INCOME STATEMENT
For 8 months ended February 28, 1997

	CURRENT MONTH			YEAR-TO-DATE		
	ACTUAL	BUDGET	VARIANCE	ACTUAL	BUDGET	VARIANCE
Sales (income)	$18,000	17,000	1,000	$144,000	136,000	8,000
Gross Profit	$18,000	17,000	1,000	144,000	136,000	8,000
Operating Expenses						
Salaries & wages	9,345	9,345	0	75,640	74,760	-880
Payroll tax/fringe	2,055	2,055	0	16,641	16,440	-201
Prof. fees	250	200	-50	2,500	1,600	-900
Rent	650	650	0	5,200	5,200	0
Utilities	35	35	0	320	280	-40
Phone/fax/cellular	225	225	0	1,960	1,800	-160
Office supplies	25	25	0	350	200	-150
Postage & delivery	103	80	-23	915	640	-275
Equipment	370	250	-120	4,200	2,000	-2200
depreciation	230	200	-30	1,900	1,600	-300
Travel/entertainment	74	100	26	678	800	122
Auto expense	286	300	14	2,288	2,400	112
Insurance	320	320	0	2,560	2,560	0
Marketing	235	280	45	2,200	2,240	40
Contributions	0	0	0	200	0	-200
Miscellaneous	118	200	82	1,020	1,600	580
Total Expenses	14,321	14,265	-56	118,572	114,120	-4452
Net Income	3,679	2,735	944	25,428	21,880	3,548

Exhibit C3

BROWDER OFFICE SUPPORT SERVICES
BALANCE SHEET
February 28, 1997

ASSETS

CURRENT ASSETS

Cash - Checking	$5,428
Cash - Savings	$20,000
Accounts Receivable	1,500
Prepaid Insurance	640
Total Current Assets	**$27,568**

FIXED ASSETS

Computer Equipment	13,000
Office Equipment	2,000
Office Furniture	8,000
Accumulated Depreciation	-9,026
Total Fixed Assets	**13,974**

OTHER ASSETS

Rent Deposit	2,000
Total Other Assets	**2,000**

TOTAL ASSETS	**$43,542**

LIABILITIES AND EQUITY

CURRENT LIABILITIES

Accounts Payable	1,731
Payroll Tax Payable	2,055
Credit Line Payable	0
Current Portion of Long-Term Debt	0
Total Current Liabilities	**$3,786**

LONG-TERM LIABILITIES

Notes Payable	0
Current Portion of Long-Term Debt	0
Total Long-Term Liabilities	**0**

EQUITY

Owner's Capital	40,328
Draws	-26,000
Retained Earnings - Current Year	25,428
Total Equity	**39,756**

TOTAL LIABILITIES AND EQUITY	**$43,542**

Amortization. The process of writing off debt for capital equipment by pro-rating the cost over a period of time, usually the life of the equipment, per government standards.

Variance. The difference between budgeted income and expenses and actual income and expenses.

Net cash flow. The balance remaining at the end of the month after expenses have been deducted from income for the month and funds available from previous month.

Net profit. The balance remaining after operating expenses and taxes have been deducted from the income for the month.

Financial Projections

A critical part of planning a business is making financial projections, or forecasting where your business will be in a year, three years, five years. Taking the time to understand how to adequately put together your financial forecast will save time, heartache and frustration by helping you to realize what your financial strengths and weaknesses are. Financial forecasting involves projecting, month by month, income and expenses as realistically as possible, so that you can begin to see that picture of where your business will be in a year and what help you might need along the way to get it to where you want it to be.

To assist you in developing your financial projections, look at Exhibits A1, A2, B1 and B2. These examples show a service business and a manufacturing business with a simple product to help you get an idea of how projecting actually works. I have broken the first year down by months for each of the two businesses, Browder Office Support Services and Susie's Silks.

You will notice in Exhibit A1 that income for Browder Office Support Services (BOSS) is made up totally of sales which, in this instance, are the sales of office support services to other businesses. The line items are on the left side with the months spread out across the page at the top. Each month indicates the total income earned for that month. Expenses are laid out and, since there are employees at BOSS, there is a line item for salaries and wages indicated as the first expense. Payroll taxes and fringe is calculated at 22% to include fringe benefits that might be paid to employees, as well as payroll taxes that must be paid to the federal government. All other items are listed according to the expenses incurred or anticipated by BOSS.

Items such as equipment and, in some instances, legal and accounting services might be prorated by the month so that you can see what the monthly expenses truly are. Notice that the owner's draw is separate from salary and wages of employees. The owner's draw, since BOSS is a sole proprietorship, is listed separately because the IRS treats all funds coming into a sole proprietorship as earnings for the owner. The owner can draw a monthly

CAUTION

SLIPPERY WHEN WET

income as long as funds are available, and then calculate the taxes due either quarterly or annually, according to IRS guidelines. BOSS has a total income of $205,000, total expenses of $164,482 and a federal income tax of $13,300. Notice that the income tax is prorated on a monthly basis.

In Exhibit A2, the cash flow projection for BOSS, actual income and actual expenses are indicated for each month. On the income and expense projection (Exhibit A1), income and expenses are indicated according to the month in which they are incurred. In other words, if you provide $18,000 worth of services in July, that is money earned for July and would appear on the income and expense projection in July. However, on cash flow projections (Exhibit A2), only that income that is received in a particular month can be listed. As with income, expenses are listed according to how they will be paid out. The reason for this will become clear in a moment.

BOSS expects that some payments to the company will not be on time and, therefore, will become receivables. So the income stated on the income and expense projection does not always match the income anticipated to be received on the cash flow projection. Notice the difference in total income between the two projections. Only $192,000 of the projected $205,000 in income is anticipated to be received during the fiscal year July 1 through June 30, and only $162,072 of the projected $164,482 in expenses is expected to actually be paid out. Also notice that the federal income tax is actually paid quarterly and is indicated accordingly on the cash flow projection. Figures are very different between the income and expenses projection and the cash flow projection.

The main purpose of performing a cash flow analysis is to determine whether:

- **You will have enough cash to meet your business obligations,**

- **You will make a profit,**

- **There will be shortfalls requiring that additional monies be available.**

To set up the cash flow projections, you need to start with a beginning balance. Show your total income, your cash flow and the net profit. The ending balance or, in this instance, the net profit is always the beginning balance for the next month. You will notice some months with a negative cash flow such as the -$401 in September. This is the difference between income and expenses for that month. In the cash flow analysis at the bottom, there is an immediate cash flow deficiency in the very first month of July because income taxes must be paid that month. While BOSS does have a net profit of $16,629, it is far less than the $27,218 net profit shown as part of the income and expenses projection. This difference occurs when monies are not received as they are earned. By completing a cash flow projection, it is easy to see whether there will be any shortfalls in cash and whether it will be necessary to have reserve funds available to see you through those shortfalls.

By making the cash flow projection, being realistic and understanding the possibility of funds not coming in as they are owed, you can begin to anticipate whether you will need a loan or to build up a reserve of money before you start the business. The projections give you the opportunity to have your business make it to the end of the first year, the second year or the third year. By performing cash flow analysis, you can stay on top of and have a finger on the pulse of your business operation, realizing months in advance the need for additional cash.

In the example of BOSS, reserve monies might be required, but because the situation is rectified in the second month, it can probably float the $940 deficit for 30 days without seriously jeopardizing its creditors or employees. BOSS would have enough money to meet its payroll. Perhaps the owner would not take as much of a draw that month in order to meet the company's burden of debt and responsibility.

In Exhibits B1 and B2, Susie's Silks, the situation is a little bit different, with income listed as Sales and Cost of Sales. The cost of sales is deducted from the actual sales to achieve gross profit. You will ordinarily see gross profit stated for businesses that produce a product, this is to show the direct related costs of producing the products sold and distinguish them from indirect costs. While on the projected income and expenses, Susie's Silks produces a total of $139,730 in income and has a net profit of $36,517, the cash flow projections are not as appealing.

The problem is that Susie's Silks gives credit to a number of customers. Many of the customers do not pay on time, so income in the cash flow projection is only $110,280, barely enough to cover incurred expenses. In the case of Susie's Silks, net income is at a deficit for the first month, yet the cash flow analysis shows a deficit for several months. Because of the burden of federal income tax, Susie's Silks is not prepared to cover the cost of all expenses in the first, fourth and seventh months.

The company begins to come out of the slump by the tenth month and is okay by the end of the year. If Susie's Silks did not have a cash reserve, the owner certainly would not be able to take a draw of $4,000 per month. That money would have to be used to cover the deficit in order to make the federal income tax payments. This would diminish the funds the owner may need to support herself. If Susie cannot cover her expenses, then her credit may be in

jeopardy. By analyzing her cash flow projection, Susie can look ahead and determine that she must have reserve funds available to meet her regular responsibilities (payables and expenses).

Far too often, small business owners allow themselves to fall into a situation where cash flow dictates that bills cannot be paid. By not paying bills or not discussing difficulties paying the bills with creditors, the credit situation for the company, as well as for the individual, becomes seriously jeopardized. In the first year of operation, small businesses have a difficult time borrowing money from a bank, especially if they do not own real estate with sufficient equity. Even if you do have real estate and equity, if your projections indicate an inability to support the loan payments, the chances of getting the loan are not likely, even if you have been in business for two or three years.

Having projections allows you to foresee problems and alleviate them by borrowing from a friend or a family member or getting a line of credit (which is often as difficult as getting a bank loan). Without projections, business owners move blindly into an abyss that can suck them up, sometimes never to be heard from again. It certainly reduces the opportunity to move forward on solid ground and to build a strong, viable business.

Second and third year projections can be done on a quarterly basis. Do the month-by-month scenario, then combine it into quarters to see what to anticipate on a quarterly basis. Continue to complete cash flow projections to give you a sense of where your income will come from and whether it will be available to you. Note that both BOSS and Susie's Silks ended up with a net profit, showing they generated enough money over 12 months to cover all expenses with money left over. But that is not always the issue.

The issue is, will you have enough money to cover your monthly expenses and avoid jeopardizing your credit or going out of business before you can collect the money owed you. Projecting income, expenses, and cash flow for at least three years will put you in control of your business. Working smart, understanding what your needs are and determining what you have to do to get those needs met, will allow you to have a functioning business.

Financial forecasting should be completed every year, not just the first. By continuing to do financial forecasting, you will maintain an uncommon but critical level of control over your business. Forecasting allows you to anticipate and to be prepared for what is coming.

Financial Reports

Once you are in business, maintaining financial statements on a regular basis is absolutely necessary to control your operation, rather than it controlling you.

Financial statements include both a balance sheet and an income statement. They show past and current accounting of the operations of the business. A balance sheet is a snapshot of a business at a particular point in time, showing assets and liabilities or claims against it, including the claims of its owner, or owner's equity. The income statement is often called the profit and loss statement or the P & L statement. It shows the profit and loss for a period of time by matching income against the expenses incurred to generate that income. There are two ways to structure the income statement: "budgeted" and "percent of income." Exhibits C1-C3 show an income statement both ways, as well as a balance sheet.

Exhibit C1 is the income statement for BOSS, showing the income for eight months, ending February 28, 1997. It lists sales, gross profits, operating expenses, total expenses and net income for the current month (actual and percentage) and year-to-date. This is a very effective way of presenting an income statement. It gives you a look at what is happening for the particular month, and it shows you year-to-date information for the eight months that are listed as a part of the heading. Percentages listed are of total income. For example, the $18,000 that is shown as income for the current month is 100 percent of the income, while year-to-date $144,000 is also 100 percent of the income. Each operating expense is also listed as a percentage of total income. Thus, total expenses of $14,321 make up 79.6 percent of total income. The net income is $3,679, or 20.4 percent of total income, a good percentage of net income.

In Exhibit C2, for the same eight months ending February 28, 1997, we show actual income, budgeted income and the variance between the two. In this instance, only $17,000 was budgeted for the current month, while $18,000 was actually earned, leaving a positive variance of $1,000. As we look down the operating expenses, we see that there is some variance. For total expenses, we see that the actual is $14,321 while the budget was $14,265, resulting in a negative variance of $56. That means BOSS was over its projected budget by $56. Net income is $3,679, or $944 over the budgeted amount. Year-to-date puts things into better perspective and allows you to really see what you have compared to what you had projected. This gives you a sense of how close you came to the amount in your projections, since your projections are your budget.

In Exhibit C3, we have the balance sheet, which is a snapshot of the business on February 28, 1997. It shows the current, fixed and other assets, current and long-term liabilities, and equity, including the owner's capital, draws against equity and retained earnings from the current year. Total assets and total liabilities/equity must always be equal, according to the double-entry accounting system. Always make sure that an accountant or a bookkeeper assists you in putting your reports together, if this is not an area in which you feel comfortable. Once an accountant completes several for you and show you how to complete them, you should be able to generate your own monthly reports, especially if you have a computerized accounting program. Having financial statements arms you with information that helps you make solid business decisions. And after completing the financial statements, you can then apply financial ratios to better understand how you fare compared to the industry and industry standards.

Financial Ratios

What is a financial ratio? It is a comparison of one item with another on the balance sheet or the income statement to identify and explain the financial strengths and weaknesses of a business. There are countless financial ratios used primarily by bankers, accountants and investors to determine how your business is developing or whether it is a solid, viable business operation.

It is amazing what you can determine just by understanding how these ratios work. When you understand and apply them, you will be better prepared, armed with all the tools and ammunition necessary to operate a strong, viable business.

To determine the strength and viability of your business, it is a good idea for you to calculate some of these financial ratios on a regular basis. However, these ratios are merely tools and can be misleading unless there is sufficient evidence of all necessary factors. Discuss ratios and the use of them with your accountant to make sure you understand how best to use and interpret them for your business, based on your industry and your situation.

The most common financial ratios are current ratio, quick ratio, and ratios that measure debt to equity, average collection period and inventory turnover. Let's take them one at a time.

CURRENT RATIO. The current ratio indicates a business's ability to finance its current operation after allowing for payment of its current liabilities. The ratio is stated as:

$$\frac{\text{Current Assets}}{\text{Current Liabilities}}$$

To determine the ratio, divide current liabilities into current assets. In the case of BOSS, current assets are $27,568 and current liabilities are $3,786. If you divide the current liabilities into the current assets, you come up with 7.3. In the industry, 2.0 to 1.0 is acceptable for the current ratio, while anything over 2 is excellent and preferable. So, with a current ratio of 7.3, BOSS is really in good shape. It indicates it can finance its current operation and pay off all of its current liabilities with funds to spare.

QUICK RATIO. The quick ratio measures the ability of a business to meet its current obligations, especially its ability to convert assets into cash quickly. It also measures the ability to cover debts due within 60 to 90 days. For this ratio, 1.0 is satisfactory. The ratio is stated as:

$$\frac{\text{Current Assets - Inventories \& Prepaid Expenses}}{\text{Current Liabilities}}$$

Current liabilities would be divided into current assets minus inventories and prepaid expenses. BOSS, has current assets of $27,568 and, while it has no inventories, and prepaid expenses of $2,000. If we take $2,000 from the $27,568 it leaves us with $25,568. Current liabilities are $3,786, which is divided into the $25,568 giving us 7. BOSS's quick ratio is beyond satisfactory.

DEBT TO EQUITY. The debt-to-equity ratio shows how much of the business is owed to all creditors versus the owner. A ratio of 2.0 to 1.0 is satisfactory. This ratio is stated as:

$$\frac{\text{Total Debt}}{\text{Total Equity}}$$

Total equity would be divided into the total debt. The total debt for BOSS is $3,786 and total equity is $39,756, resulting in a ratio of 1 so BOSS again has a satisfactory rating.

AVERAGE COLLECTION PERIOD. This ratio indicates the net sales for an accounting period compared to the amount of unpaid accounts and notes receivable for that period. Thirty days is the standard in all industries. The ratio is stated as:

$$\frac{\text{Net Sales}}{\text{Receivables}}$$

To convert the answer into days, divide the answer into 360, the number of days used by financial analysts to determine a standard year. (It excludes five legal holidays.)

BOSS's net sales equal $25,428 with receivables of $1,500. The result is 16.9, which is divided into 360 to come up with an average collection period of 21 days. BOSS has a lower average collection period than the industry standard of 30 days.

INVENTORY TURNOVER. This is only done for companies that maintain inventory. This ratio indicates the rate of merchandise turnover or, how long purchased or manufactured items remain unsold. A ratio of 1.5 months to 2 months is satisfactory. The ratio is stated as:

$$\frac{\text{Cost of Goods Sold}}{\text{Inventory}}$$

Use the average of beginning and ending inventories for the month. Divide the answer by 12 to give you the average number of inventory turns in a year. Note: This ratio can be misleading if you produce a high priced, low volume inventory item that turns over only a few times a year but may have a high "markup" to account for the few turns in inventory.

By understanding these ratios and calculating them regularly, you can be as sophisticated as a banker in making decisions about your business. It will help you understand exactly where you stand and what you might need to do to be as profitable as you want.

BREAK-EVEN ANALYSIS. There is one other formula I would like to introduce here, the break-even analysis. It is not a financial ratio, but it is applied to your financial projections to get a better sense of when you can start to make a profit. Only after hitting the break-even point can you begin to achieve a profit.

The break-even point is that point at which there is no profit and no loss. As much money has been generated as capital has been put into the operation, so that you are at an even point. To use the formula, you must understand what fixed costs are as compared to variable costs. Fixed costs are those you must pay regardless of whether you are generating any revenue. Rent is a fixed cost. Utilities, phone bills, office supplies and insurance are all fixed costs. These must be paid regardless.

Variable costs, on the other hand, are those that vary according to revenue generated. If you need to spend money on marketing to maintain a high level of revenue, then marketing is a variable expense. Other variable expenses might be salaries and wages (other than for yourself), as well as payroll taxes and fringe benefits. Professional fees are variable if they depend on whether you are generating the revenue to necessitate professional services. Travel, entertainment and sometimes auto expenses are variable expenses. The formula for determining the break-even point is:

$$\frac{\text{Total Fixed Costs}}{1 - [\text{Total Variable Costs} / \text{Total Sales}]}$$

BOSS's fixed costs are: rent, utilities, phone, postage, equipment, depreciation, insurance and accounting services, which total $22,530 (Exhibit A1). The variable costs are: salaries, fringe benefits, office expenses, travel, auto, marketing, legal services, contributions, miscellaneous and owner's draw, totaling $141,952. To set up the calculation, the total sales ($205,000) are divided into $141,952, which equals 1.44. This total is subtracted from 1 and then divided into $22,530 (fixed costs). The result is $51,204. This is the amount of revenue that must be generated before a profit can begin to be achieved. Only after earning $51,204 can there be hope of making a profit. The break-even in this example would be achieved in BOSS's third month of operation for this particular year.

Here are a few helpful tips. On a monthly basis, you should:

- **Compare your sales (your income) and your expenses to the budget. Identify past-due receivables and take corrective action. Conduct ratio analysis to determine your financial weaknesses in the business. Check entries on the balance sheet to make sure that they agree with totals in the ledger, as this is a way of double-checking yourself.**

- **Confirm that prepaid expenses are posted properly. Accountants tell me that this is one of the most common errors that microbusinesses make. Without a review of financial information by accountants, this error can go unchecked. Prepaid expenses is a special category that must be posted to your balance properly so that it does not cause you an extra tax burden.**

- **Have an accountant review your accounting on a regular basis to make sure that your records are accurate.**

It is your money that you are working hard to earn. You do not want to lose your money or pay more in taxes than you should just because you have not kept proper accounting records. Save your receipts and make sure that you can justify all expenses by attaching a receipt of some sort to each (canceled) check written. Take the time to take care of your business.

Establishing a Relationship With a Bank

Most business owners have checking accounts, but all too often they do their banking across the counter with a teller and do not bother to ever establish a relationship with a bank officer. The time to establish a relationship is right at the beginning, when you don't even need a loan or when you cannot yet get one. Take the time, even in selecting a bank, to find one person at that bank with whom you can develop a rapport.

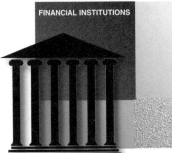

FINANCIAL INSTITUTIONS

Even before you open a checking account, talk to various bankers at different banks to see which one you are comfortable with. Which one do you feel is going to be more understanding of microbusinesses? Do they know what you go through, and will they be sympathetic when needed? Determine which bank you will put your money in by the rapport you can establish with a banker.

If there are problems with a bank once you have established an account, go to the banker with whom you have hopefully established a rapport, and ask your questions. If the bank is charging fees higher than you want or if you do not understand the fees you are being assessed, it is helpful to have one person with whom you can talk.

Make sure that you know exactly what you need to ask of this person so that you can get good information. Make sure your questions get answered and that the answer is directly related to what you need to find out. If a bank cannot address the questions and concerns that you have, for whatever reason, do not hesitate for one moment to change your account. A relationship with a banker is far more important than staying with a bank that is not treating you properly. If the banker you have established a relationship with moves to another bank, consider moving your account to the other bank. That banker will take care of you. For example, if you need a loan, even if you are not totally qualified for one, having a rapport with that banker could give you the edge you need to get that loan approved. Don't count on this, but it is something you should strive for, should you ever need it.

Once you have established a rapport, make sure to visit the banker regularly. It is not enough to talk just when you open the account. Make it a point to talk regularly. Bankers can get information for you that you cannot always get for yourself. Having a relationship with a banker often gives you access to industry information that may not be easily available at a library.

Robert Morris & Associates is a firm out of Philadelphia that provides all kinds of industry information and reports. If you cannot find the information in the library, it will cost you money to access these reports. Banks have them as a normal course of business. There is also other information that comes across a banker's desk or that they know just as a matter of course. By establishing a rapport, you can be privy to this information that can ultimately help you to be more effective in running your business.

Do not get caught up in the day-to-day workings of your business so much so that you do not get out or take the time to make phone calls to maintain relationships once they are established. Remember: The relationship with a banker can be one of the most important relationships you can establish in the course of operating your business.

STRATEGIC PLAN OUTLINE

A strategic plan is an expanded business plan. It specifically spells out all the strategies for accomplishing the goals and objectives of the organization, and it details the business structure and succession plan for the owners. Attention is given to operational system design for uniformity of business operations.

Should a need arise for financing, a business plan can be easily extracted from the information contained in this plan.

The following outline will assist you in developing your thoughts to create a strong plan that will give you a sense of direction for your business. Remember, you always plan—you either plan to succeed or you plan to fail. The choice is yours.

Executive Summary
An overview of the business plan, always written last but positioned at beginning,

The Company
Purpose Statement (Who are you? (business) What do you do? For whom do you do it? What is the benefit derived by customer/client?

Mission Statement (A never-ending quest to achieve a broad goal for the business)

Company History
How old is the firm (use dates rather than number if years)? Why was it started? What is present focus?

Feasibility
What is result of research? Does it make sense to operate and why? Will people buy at estimated price and why? Who will buy? How far will they come for the product or service?

Goals
Short-term—less than two years. List SMART goals with objectives, not strategies.

Long-term—more than two years. List SMART goals with objectives, not strategies.

Management Team
Discussion of owners, managers, qualifications/experience, separation of responsibilities.

Personal Objectives of Management
Personal goals of owner(s), impact these goals expected to have on business, strategies for fulfilling goals.

Organizational Structure

Current situation, employees, anticipated growth pattern, number of employees, classification, responsibilities, need for and anticipated contribution to company

(Design organizational chart based on five-year anticipated growth pattern.)

Succession

Who will run company upon demise or incapacitation of current owner(s); plan is necessary.

SWOT Elements

Strengths—What strengths exist in current or planned structure? Which will benefit you in reaching goals or will provide advantages?

Weaknesses—What weaknesses must be overcome, or what disadvantages exist that will impact the business? What can be/will be done to eliminate these negatives?

Opportunities—What external situations will positively impact on the accomplishment of the goals (clout or contacts)?

Threats—What external factors might impact the business negatively (often beyond your control such as the economy, etc.). What might you do to either avoid the threats or deal with them effectively to minimize the effects?

Industry Data and Competition

Industry—What industry? What benefits do users derive? What is the industry's annual revenue? What is the current status of industry? What trends exist now and in the near future (two years)? What long-term trends are anticipated? What are projected sales for the industry over the next five years?

Competition—Who are competitors serving the same market segment? What are strategies used by competition? What rates/prices do competitors charge? What differences exist between you and the competition? What is market share of the competition (if possible)?

Market Information

Identify target markets, any niches. Discuss strategies for reaching target markets according to SMART guidelines.

Product/Service

Discuss your operations concept. Why do you operate as you do in the business? What are your philosophies for providing services or producing products? How do the methods serve clients/customers? How do you measure your performance (some mechanism is necessary)? What triggers will be used to determine if improvements are needed?

Price/Fee Structure

Current price/fee, method for determining the price/fee and how any adjustments will be made in the future.

Credit Policy

What guidelines will be implemented if credit is to be issued? Collection procedures? Interest to be charged? Will there be late charges?

Sales Strategies

Discuss strategies for accomplishing sales goals and objectives. Discuss any in-house support to be utilized. Are there any pre-sale costs?

Manufacturing Considerations

Discuss equipment, layout, tooling, production information, limitations, scheduling, packaging, shipping, etc. What kind of inspection systems (quality control) will there be? How will you handle inventory controls?

Retail Operation

What is the nature of your shop? What kind of budgets will you develop? How will you handle inventory control? What is your purchasing strategy? Will you use "open-to-buy" systems? How will you deal with theft/pilferage? What security measures will you take?

Operational System Design

What procedures will you follow in handling business matters? (Specific systems must be designed and used consistently to ensure uniformity in operations.) How will you collect and analyze data to assist in making good business decisions? What business forms will you develop and use? How will you measure where you are in accomplishing your goals? What standards will you use to hire and manage employees, sub-contractors? How will you handle customer service?

Operational Controls

Once systems are in place, how will you monitor to make sure they are being followed? What controls will you used for reporting purposes? How will you use performance evaluations, currently and in the future? Will customers complete evaluations on your service or products?

Pro Forma

Financial Projections—Complete for three-to-five years. Do month-by-month for year one and by quarters for year two and later. Explain reasoning for figures used (assumptions/footnotes).

Cash Flow Analysis—Complete yearly analysis of cash flow to determine if any shortfalls are present and when. Be realistic about when funds will be received and paid.

Break-Even Analysis—Using formula, determine when income will equal what has been spent to capitalize and operate the business.

Return on Investment—Also using formula, determine the return on investment for the first year of operation.

Financial Statements—If currently in business, include current financial reports (balance sheet, income statement). Profit and Loss Statement is same as income statement.

OPERATIONAL/ORGANIZATIONAL SYSTEMS

Contrary to popular (uninformed) belief, small and micro business-es need to have operational systems to avoid problems as they grow. Systems form the infrastructure for a business, allowing a foundation to be laid that will facilitate growth rather than inhibit it. Failure to develop and implement functional systems initially, will force a business to a screeching halt once it does start to grow; peak productivity cannot be achieved without them.

Following are a few systems that will allow you to "work smart," preserving your energy and maximizing productivity. Develop and re-design systems as necessary to meet the needs of your business. Designing these systems with the future in mind is the key.

INFORMATIONAL SYSTEMS
Data collection (detailed information on clients/customers, ven-dors, employees and contractors)

- forms
- reports
- logs
- questionnaires

Evaluation forms
- internal
- external

General recordkeeping systems
- correspondence files
- associates(info about them)
- networking materials collected
- administrative files
- business records (licenses, registrations, articles of incorporation, etc.)
- market research results
- competition files
- resources
- documents

OPERATIONAL SYSTEMS
Accounting systems

- budgets
- journal
- inventory control
- tax payments
- petty cash records
- accounts payable
- check writing
- ledger
- financial reports
- cancelled checks
- accounts receivable

Pricing/fee setting system
- cost analysis records
- guidelines for increasing or decreasing prices/fees

Purchasing system (retail in particular)
- plans for purchasing
- open-to-buy structure
- annual budget

Security system
- protection of business ideas
- servicemarks
- safe, if necessary
- trademarks
- copyrights
- locked files, desks

POLICIES AND PROCEDURES (Processes and guidelines for operating a business effectively)

Employees/Contractors
- job descriptions (including yours)
- performance evaluations
- time sheets
- benefits structure
- dress code
- vacation structure/guidelines
- agreements (if necessary)
- reporting requirements
- pay structure
- pay periods
- attendance policies
- training schedule/policy
- hiring policies

Clients/customers
- limits in dealing with a client/customer
- expectations of each party
- customer service guidelines
- quality assurance
- guarantee/warranty policies
- return policies
- shipping/handling guidelines
- constructive feedback (evaluation of your performance)

Credit policy
- terms (discount structure, interest rate/late fee)
- collection procedure

Vendors/suppliers
Guidelines for dealing with suppliers (Such as, who can be authorized to initiate an order, etc.)

These are but a few of the various systems that can assist you in operating your business efficiently and profitably. The type of system is not as important as whether it will provide you the kind of information or guidelines that help you to be productive.

Creating a system means you do it once (think it and write it). Then you don't have to think about it anymore, which frees you to focus on your bottom line rather than on putting out fires.

To maintain their effectiveness, systems must be adjusted as circumstances dictate to keep in step with changing times.

PRESS RELEASE

(TO BE WRITTEN ON LETTERHEAD)

Contact: Name,
Phone

<u>FOR IMMEDIATE RELEASE</u>

"PRESERVE YOUR HISTORY" TRAINING TO START

Remember Forever, a local organization working to preserve modern history, will sponsor a 20-hour training program to teach interested individuals how to preserve photographs and papers for future generations. Classes will be held at the Luther Park Community Center and will begin on Tuesday, March 20 at 6:00 PM. Classes will run each Tuesday for five weeks. The cost is $45.

Classes are open to senior citizens as well as children and all ages in between. Proceeds from the class will be used to assist Remember Forever in their effort to purchase materials used to help terminally ill children to create archive quality photo albums of themselves for their families.

The instructor for the class is Susie Cue, owner of Susie's Silks, a silk floral design firm. Ms. Cue taught photo and document preservation for ten years at ABC University prior to starting the floral design business. Ms. Cue frequently donates her time to aid sick children.

To register for the classes or for additional information, call Jan at Remember Forever, 111-222-3333 or stop by their offices at 1234 Main St, 1st floor. The deadline for registration is March 10.

- 30 -

BROWDER OFFICE SUPPORT SERVICES
COST ANALYSIS, SERVICE
1996

Salary/fringe (22%), three empl, + you	$11,400
Rent (% of home used or rented office)	650
Utilities	35
Phone/cell phone/fax/pager	225
Postage	58
Office supplies	25
Frieght, shipping	45
Stationery/brochures/cards	49
Marketing/networking/dues/membership	235
Subcriptions	4
Insurance; car, bus-liability, health-life	320
Car expense,(pro-rated for use)	286
Travel, mileage-$.30 per mile	74
Copies/printing	65
Accountant, pro-rated	50
Legal services, pro-rated	50
Equipment, pro-rated	120
Computers, printers, pro-rated	250
Office furniture, pro-rated	85
Contingency	500
Subtotal	$14,526
Profit (15%)	2,179
TOTAL	$16,705

Total divided by 275 billable hrs. per mo.

$61 Hrly billing rate

SUSIE'S SILKS
COST ANALYSIS MODEL, PRODUCTS
1996

Raw materials	$2,240
Other materials/supplies	1,460
Tools, pro-rated	4
Equipment, pro-rated	2
Office furniture, pro-rated	85
Computer, printer, pro-rated	65
Rent, % of home used	232
Utilities	25
Car expenses, 80% of use	260
Insurance; car, bus-liability, health-life	250
Stationery/brochures/cards	24
Marketing/networking/dues/memberships	300
Subcriptions	4
Phone/cell phone/fax	150
Postage	64
Travel, mileage-$.30 per mile	74
Copies/printing	65
Accountant, pro-rated	50
Legal services, pro-rated	50
Shipping	86
Salary/fringe, (22%), owner	4,000
Contingency	500
Subtotal	$9,990
Profit (25%)	2,498
TOTAL	$12,488

Total divided by 300 silk floral units $42 Avr. price per unit

Protection Of Intellectual Property

Copyrights. A copyright is a protection offered for intellectual property. This category applies to written material, music (lyrics and composition), and some art forms such as photography and sculptures. The protection is offered through the federal government as well as through a cooperative agreement with other nations in the world.

While there is no requirement to register a body of work for a copyright, federal law does require that all written or musical bodies of work be submitted to the Library of Congress, copyright office once it is published, as a matter of record. If published works are not submitted, a penalty may result. Registering the copyright establishes ownership, thus providing protection should there ever arise a question of when it was written and by whom. Mandatory submission only provides the government with a record of what is being published but does not protect the owner of the property unless it is also registered. For additional information contact:

    Library of Congress, Copyright Office
    101 Independence Avenue, S.E.
    Washington, D.C. 20559-6000
    202-707-3000

Trademarks. A trademark is also a form of protection for intellectual property. In this instance the property would be a word, group of words (jingle, tagline, et al), a name, logo or symbol. Registration of the word, words, logo or symbol provides protection against someone else using the same item in the same style or form as registered. A trademark is used on items which are sold ("traded").

A servicemark, often used interchangeably with trademark, is actually designated for names or symbols of services. Application for trademark or servicemark is voluntary. The cost is $245 per registration as of 1997. For additional information about trademarks and servicemarks contact:

    Patents and Trademarks
    Commissioner of Patents
    Washington, D.C. 20231
    703-557-3158

Patents. A patent is still another form of protection for intellectual property. Patents cover things, such as inventions or technologies. Patents are very complicated and require the assistance of a skilled attorney to assist in the application process. Patents cover the research and development of an item or process as well as all the specifications involved in reproducing the same. Often the patent process takes years due to all the intricate details which must be addressed. Searches must be conducted to make sure no one else has such a patent and prototypes must be tested to make sure the invention or technology works. For additional information on patents contact:

Patents and Trademarks
Commissioner of Patents
Washington, D.C. 20231
703-557-3158

Gerri Norington started her first venture in 1968, subcontracting to consulting firms catering to small businesses. Initially writing sales training materials and telemarketing scripts, Gerri eventually began working directly with microbusiness owners to teach them to be efficient and profitable in running their businesses. This, long before microbusinesses were recognized as distinct from small businesses.

Gerri has owned and operated five businesses, additionally maintaining the consulting practice. These businesses included several marketing companies and a manufacturing operation with 18 employees. For four years during the 1980's, she developed and taught business development courses at seven colleges and universities in Chicago, while continuing to operate her businesses. By the mid-80s, Gerri had developed a comprehensive microbusiness training program now known as the ROSE Program™ (The Road To Self-Employment).

Gerri is the author of more than forty business advice columns called, *Taking Care Of Business*, which she wrote for two national magazines under her byline. She has founded two nonprofit business assistance centers: Entrepreneurial Training and Assistance Center in Chicago, and the Women's Business Training Center in San Diego, and has assisted thousands of small and micro businesses owners over the years.

She is the author of *"...Built With Confidence"*, *The Money-Making Guide for Small Business Owners*, a 6-hour audio program with a 16-page workbook.

Gerri is divorced, has a daughter, Karin, a practicing attorney in Baltimore, whom she raised as a single-parent while struggling as an entrepreneur.